The Love of Living Foods

Robin Gregory

DEDICATION

This book is dedicated to my Mom, my greatest source of inspiration, who gave me an appreciation of life, art and beauty and who has been my companion on this raw food journey and through life.

CONTENTS

ACKNOWLEDGMENTS

I would like to thank all of my family, friends and closest loved ones for supporting me and encouraging me to follow my passion, to my kids Dylan, Nick and Kaiya for being wonderful and inspiring to me also, to Jim, Lisa, Danny and all of the Robinsons. I would like to thank the countless predeceasing raw food gurus who have taken this journey before and especially those who have shared their knowledge and wisdom with others, so it could trickle down to me. I would like to thank all of my contemporaries on the raw food path and all of the teachers and people who share their wisdom and time to enlighten the world on this lighter, more sustainable, healthier and compassionate way of life. Special thanks to Marie Larsson, TD, Victoria Boutenko, David Wolfe, Jinjee and Storm Talifero, Angela Stokes and Matt Monarch, Pierce and Sheryl, Nomi Shannon, Sarma Melngailis, Dr. Brian and Anna Maria Clement, Dr. Doug Graham, Dorit, Juliano, Chad Sarno, Matthew Kenney, Terces Engelhart, Renée Underkoffler and to all of the raw food chefs and people working in raw food kitchens, because I know how much work and dedication it takes to go against the grain, to follow your passion and to help others to heal themselves and lead happier, more productive and exciting lives. It is truly a wonderful thing, and so Thank you!

1 FORWARD

Creating dishes using raw foods is an exciting experience. Although there are new techniques to learn and use such as dehydrating, blending and soaking nuts and seeds, once you get familiar with these, you will find creating raw dishes fun, easy and quick. People are delightfully surprised at how easy it is to prepare raw dishes. Kids usually love it and are naturally drawn to and adept at becoming creative raw chefs.

A benefit of creating raw dishes is that the base you are working with is comprised of flavors in their pure state. Just as it is easier for an artist to create rich colors using natural pure pigments, similarly, a chef will have an advantage using the pure flavors of food in its natural state. A wonderful aspect of working with raw foods is the way the flavors blend and develop together. Experimenting usually leads to delightful surprises and no matter how creative one gets the outcome is often a successful one.

While many raw food recipes are unique there are also many which are made to approximate traditional cooked food dishes. This creates a familiarity with our food, a comfort and also creates a base to understand the nature of working with foods in their pure state leaving us enabled to move on with knowledge to develop more uniquely raw creations. It is also just fun to create a raw apple pie, or cheesecake, for example, which rivals any cooked one, even and often to master chefs and connoisseurs of cooked foods.

Creating and experimenting with traditional dishes as well as world cuisine flavors is an exciting and rewarding challenge. My aim is to only create dishes that are as good as our traditional cooked ones and also that supersede them, so that we are able to enjoy dishes that are great for our body and our soul and are great for our sensual experience also. I love to share my creations with others and it is a pleasure to share these recipes with you to enjoy the experience of these taste sensations in a wholly natural and health enhancing way.

I wish you bliss and happiness.
To your health, with love!
Robin Gregory

2 FOOD PREPARATION TECHNIQUES

There are a few new techniques to learn and get to know when starting to create in a raw kitchen. In addition to useful tips given in the equipment and ingredient sections, extra tips and information are given here.

Soaking - Soaking awakens nuts, seeds and grains from their dormant state. As they begin to grow the energy and vitality is increased in them; they now become a 'live' food. Kirlian photography clearly shows this - with the soaked seed having a bright aura around it, while the dormant seed has none. Soaking removes their enzyme inhibitors - this is the protective shield, which Mother Nature has placed around them to prevent them from growing until they have found a place in the earth and a source of water. Removing these inhibitors releases the enzymes contained within them, which they need to grow, which are also the same ones our body uses to digest them.

Soaking removes oxylates and phytates, which keeps the minerals 'locked up' in the seed. It makes these minerals, not only more available and accessible, but more easily absorbed by the body. Soaking also increases the vitamin content.

Seeds, nuts and grains which have been soaked are much easier to digest as this process begins the digestion process by turning fats into fatty acids, transforming starches into simple sugars, and breaking proteins down into amino acids. I know of people who are allergic to

3

nuts who can comfortably eat them with no allergic symptoms when they are soaked first. This process of soaking nuts and seeds also makes them more alkaline, which is beneficial to our bodies. Soaking also reduces calories.

General guidelines for Soaking Nuts and Seeds

Use pure or filtered water to soak.

Rinse well after soaking. The soak water will still contain the released enzyme inhibitors, which are toxic, very acidic and which will neutralize our body's own store of enzymes.

Very soft or mucilaginous nuts and seeds are not soaked prior to using them in recipes, unless indicated; these include: macadamia, pine and Brazil nuts and, flax and chia seeds.

All others are soaked unless specified otherwise.

Soaking Guideline

Small seeds, grains and soft nuts, such as sesame, quinoa, walnuts and pecans – **Soak 3 to 4 hours**

Larger, hulled seeds, such as pumpkin and sunflower seeds – **Soak 4 to 8 hours**

Larger nuts, such as almonds and hazelnuts – **Soak 8 to 12 hours**

Almonds are great to have readily available and can be soaked for up to a week in the fridge. Rinse and cover with water in a glass jar and place in the fridge. Leave them without a lid, so they can breathe. Rinse then daily, as they are alive and produce waste, which will get in the water. Fill bottle with water again after and return to fridge.

If you require a shorter soaking time soak nuts and seeds in warm water. This can speed up the process by an hour or two. Heat water up until just warm to the touch; if the water is too hot for your hand, it's too hot for the food and will begin destroying beneficial nutrients and enzymes.

Sprouting - Seeds which have been sprouted are at the peak of their nutritional value. Nutrients and vitamins found only in trace amounts in the seed are multiplied during sprouting. They have dramatically increased nutrient and enzyme levels. They are the most concentrated source of vitamins, minerals, amino acids (protein), and enzymes, of any known food. Sprouts are loaded with protein in a form that is easy for the body to use and are low in fat, with no saturated fats or cholesterol. Also, as shown by Kirlian photography, sprouts have a huge life-force energy field around them which is transferred to your own body when eaten.

Sprouts grow quickly, take only a few days to grow, and are convenient. They can be grown indoors and don't take a lot of space. It's easy!

General Instructions for Sprouting - Jar method

Soak 2 to 4 tablespoons of seeds in a clean, sterilized, wide mouth jar. Fill jar half-way with water and let sit for required time, approximately 4 to 6 hours for smaller seeds and up to 12 hours for larger seeds and beans.

Cover jar with mesh screen or cheesecloth, secured with a rubber band and drain. Invert jar and prop at an angle in a bowl or on a rack. But be careful to drain thoroughly before inverting in bowl - sitting in a puddle is the most common cause of crop failure.

Rinse twice a day. Fill jar with water, swirl and drain. Rinsing removes waste products produced by the sprouts. Set jar back, at an angle, in bowl or rack.

Sprouts are ready in 3 to 6 days. Transfer to another clean jar with a lid or a re-sealable plastic bag and store in the refrigerator. Make sure they are well drained and fairly dry before storing. They should keep well for at least 7 to 10 days in the refrigerator.

Dehydrating - Dehydrating is a way of preserving and changing the texture of foods by removing water from them. The warm temperature in the dehydrator draws the moisture out of food into the air while the air currents from the fan speed up drying by moving the moist air away from the food.

Dehydrated foods, while still alive and raw, are not as healthy as unprocessed whole foods. However, they can be great for transitioning to a raw diet, providing a link between cooked and raw foods. They are also good for providing denser, more filling foods that will stay with you longer. The longer food is dried and the higher the temperature that food is dried at, the more life force and nutrients will be lost. Dehydrate below 115 degrees as enzymes are destroyed above this temperature.

Dehydrators are useful for creating many raw recipes, such as: breads, crackers, burgers, patties, cereals, cookies, etc. They are also great for preserving and drying natural plant foods, such as: tomatoes, apples, bananas, apricots, etc. Dehydrating can be used to marinate vegetable entrees. Vegetables will absorb a marinade quicker and soften slightly in the dehydrator. It is also great for heating foods.

Drying foods is a slow process, often taking up to a day or even longer. The drying time will depend on the type of food, its thickness and how dry you want it to be. Be patient. Do not try to speed up time by turning up the heat - this not only harms valuable nutrients.

After drying allow a cooling period of 30 minutes to an hour to prevent condensation.

Beware of commercially dried foods. These often contain sulfur dioxide, sodium bisulfate, refined sugar and other chemicals, which help to retard spoilage but are harmful to our health.

Dehydrated foods will keep for long periods of time. Depending on the food and the amount it is dried, most foods will keep for a month or longer with proper storage. Store dehydrated foods in an air-tight container or zip-lock bag in the coolest, darkest, driest place you can find. They can be stored well in the refrigerator and most can be frozen for even longer storage.

Fermenting - is a process in which foods are predigested creating an abundance of friendly bacteria and enzymes. Many of the civilizations and cultures in the world which were the longest living included fermented foods as a staple part of their diet. There are many fermented foods which can be included in the raw diet, including: nut cheeses, kimchi, sauerkraut, rejuvelac, kombucha, miso and nama shoyu. Eating these foods is very beneficial to the body. They are known to strengthen the immune system, protect the inner linings of the intestines and aid in the digestive process. Also the good bacteria in fermented foods help to prevent overgrowths of harmful bacteria and fungus.

Heating - Some meals are just nicer to have hot, especially in colder climates. Recipes can be heated up if desired by placing a bowl over a pot of boiling water. Stir often to make sure the underneath does not get too hot and finger test and watch carefully to heat just enough to make warm. The whole idea is to keep the food 'living' and if it is too hot, and will harm you, it will also harm the life-force energy in the food. Remember that chilling mellows flavors and warming brings flavors out. Most foods are better served at room temperature than straight out of the fridge. To do so you can heat up over hot water or by placing in a dehydrator or by allowing enough time for the food to sit out of the fridge to come up to room temperature naturally.

3 EQUIPMENT FOR THE RAW KITCHEN

Blender - This is essential in a raw kitchen for blending soups, smoothies, dressings, sauces and anything that requires a smooth texture or is of a liquid consistency. A standard home blender ($50 to 100) will work fine to start with but you may wish, eventually, to invest in a powerful high-speed blender such as a Blendtec or a Vita-Mix. These blenders have more powerful motors, long warranties and will last for many years. They are fairly expensive ($400 to 700) but most raw foodists use them regularly, at least once if not several times a day. This is my favorite kitchen appliance. It makes food preparation easy and the quality of blended foods is much higher.

Dehydrator - These have many uses from drying fruits and vegetables in season to making various raw foods such as breads, crackers, fruit leather, cookies and bars. When buying a dehydrator make sure to buy one with a fan and a temperature control. The Excalibur makes great home dehydrators in 4, 5 and 9 tray models. The 4 tray has 4 - 9" x 9" screens and the 5 and 9 tray models have larger 14" x 14" screens. The 9 tray is the most popular and most cost effective one but the 4 tray is great for limited spaces. When purchasing a dehydrator make sure to also buy teflex sheets. They are sold separately and very useful, most recipes start with drying on the teflex sheet and then transferring to the mesh dehydrator screen.

Food Processor - This is useful for blending and chopping foods. These are found in most department and kitchen stores and any quality one will work fine. They usually come with attachment blades for slicing, grating and shredding foods but the main S-blade is the one most often used for blending and chopping foods from a coarse to a very fine texture. A small $35 to $50 counter processor is a good idea to have. It is useful for smaller jobs and for easy clean-up.

Ice Cream Maker – is a manual or electric machine which is used to make small quantities, usually 1 ½ to 2 quarts of ice cream at home. Most ice cream makers on the market today chill the ice cream mixture in a container which has been cooled in the freezer, and simultaneously stirs and churns the mixture to prevent the formation of ice crystals and aerates it to create a smooth creamy consistency. Most of these counter top models require the ice cream to be frozen an extra few hours in the freezer for the ice cream to harden to a desired consistency to serve. Home ice cream makers are available in most of the larger kitchen and department stores.

Juicer – When choosing a juicer, select either a single auger or twin gear juicer, such as the Omega or Green Star. While more expensive than the more common centrifugal juicers, the price is well worth it. Both operate at low speeds, 70 to 120 rpm, and the produce is crushed which preserves the enzymes and nutrients, as opposed to the fast spinning centrifugal juicers. These machines produce the highest quality juice, they have a high juice yield and juice leafy greens well, including wheatgrass. These machines have other functions also: they have pasta extractor nozzles, they grind vegetables and nuts, and they make great nut butters, baby food and amazing frozen banana 'ice-cream'. These are by far the easiest of all juicers to clean.

Spiral Slicer - Inexpensive ($25 to 35) spiralizers break easily and do not always work very well. I have and regularly use the Spirooli and the Benreiner spiralizers, which can be found at many specialty kitchen stores. These are more expensive (50 to 100$ and up) and have a straight blade and several attachment blades for various size noodles. Zucchini put through these machines with the correct blade makes incredible raw spaghetti. This is not the most essential item to purchase in stocking a raw kitchen but is definitely a great asset and fun to have.

Spice (Coffee) Grinder - These are inexpensive ($20 to 40) small electrical counter grinders which are great for grinding small amounts of nuts, seeds or spices. If you have one which you use to grind coffee, I would advise getting another specifically for spices and seeds.

Mesh Nut Milk Bag - These are great for straining nut milks. Cheesecloth and strainers will also work but they are messier to use. The mesh bags are inexpensive and can be washed and reused.

Mandolin - is useful for cutting fruits and vegetables into uniformly thin slices or julienned strips and, while not essential, is especially useful when making large quantities of food.

Knives - Good sharp knives are essential. Have at least one high quality Chef's knife and paring knife. A Japanese cleaver is handy to have for opening young coconuts.

Whetstone or **Sharpening Tool** - for sharpening knives.

Lemon Juicer (Reamer) - A small hand juicer will work fine and be used often.

Salt Grinder – Although not essential, freshly ground coarse Celtic salt is wonderful.

Cutting Board - Non-toxic, bamboo is great.

Strainers - There are two good strainers which are both useful to have. A large metal fine mesh screen sieve strainer is very versatile and useful for straining liquids as well as for sprouting buckwheat or quinoa in. A larger stainless steel colander with slightly bigger holes and which can sit in the sink can be useful for straining larger quantities of nuts and seeds and washing vegetables.

Vegetable Peeler - Get the best quality vegetable peeler you can find.

This is an often used utensil in a raw kitchen and it makes life so pleasurable to have a really good one.

Vegetable Grater – A small zest grater or micro plane is helpful for grating orange and lemon zest and for finely grating. Most other grating can be done in the food processor with the grating attachment; this is especially helpful when making larger amounts.

A Water Filter – is very important for clean water, unless you have access to fresh spring or mountain water.

4 TIPS

Substituting Ingredients - is generally a safe thing to do in raw recipes. Here are a few guidelines to follow. Also, look in the ingredient section also for more ideas on substituting and for information on specific ingredients.

Nuts and seeds - can generally be substituted. Try to substitute the one asked for in a recipe for another similar in taste or texture. If you are out of sunflower seeds, try almonds or cashews or vice versa. Pecans can substitute well for walnuts. Sesame seeds can work for hemp seeds in small quantities but sometimes not in larger amounts as hemp seeds have a higher oil content. Flax produces a gelatinous, binding quality when wet and can often be substituted with chia seeds.

Fruits - Using different fruits or berries can often be done without compromising the dish. However, when you do this use fruits that are similar in their texture and consistency; mangoes and bananas are both thick and creamy when blended and pears substitute well for apples. Generally berries can substitute well for one another.

Cacao – Raw cacao is sold as a powder, as a fresh ground solid mass and as nibs. The nibs can be ground to substitute for chocolate powder in recipes and solid cacao mass can be melted. Sometimes cacao powder is sold with the cacao butter (the oil or fat of the cacao bean) taken out. The recipes in this book are always better with the inclusion of the cacao butter, which has much of the taste and also gives the rich texture we generally desire when eating chocolate.

Carob, which is also available raw - the ground powder from the pods of the carob (St John's fruit) tree, can also be substituted, but will have a different flavor than cacao.

Cocoa powder usually refers to cacao beans which have been roasted and then ground. Cocoa generally has a stronger flavor but it is not raw and therefore loses much of the superfood qualities of the original cacao bean. However, in terms of flavor, cocoa can be substituted for cacao in recipes.

Herbs and Spices - Dried herbs can generally be substituted for fresh. If the recipe asks for fresh herbs, use half the required amount of dried, as fresh dried herbs are quite concentrated. However, take into account the freshness of the dried herbs when substituting as they can lose much of their flavor over time.

Raw sweeteners - can easily be substituted for each other. Some people prefer not to eat honey or maple syrup, which is not raw but which sometimes may be used for flavor. Usually these are interchangeable and instead of using either you can use agave or dates or both. Substitute and use an equal amount of agave for honey or maple syrup in any recipe and vice versa. Raisins can usually be suitably substituted for dates and both can be made into a paste by blending with water. This paste can be used substituted for honey, maple syrup or agave. When using different sweeteners keep in mind that although these will all give similar levels of sweetness, the flavor will be affected, so make sure that the flavor of the substituted ingredient also will enhance and compliment the other ingredients in the recipe.

Vinegar – Apple Cider vinegar is classified as the only raw vinegar available and usually it is safe to substitute apple cider vinegar in recipes for balsamic and other vinegars to keep it completely raw, the only difference will be a slight taste variance. In salad dressings, lemon can often be substituted for any vinegar.

It does not take long to get a feel for alternatives to use and you may wish to experiment. This is sometimes how great dishes are created.

Consistency and adding liquids to recipes – This especially refers to making sauces, soups, smoothies and recipes of a more liquid consistency. When a recipe asks for water or liquid to be added, use some caution and go more on the side of less liquid first. More can always be added but it is hard to remove once too much liquid is put in. In cooking you can boil things down to remove water, but when creating with raw foods, the process is usually blending or processing and this cannot be done. However, it doesn't take long to understand the nature of raw foods and a correct judgment call will soon come naturally.

Flavor variances in recipes - Each time you make something it will taste slightly different. Have you ever noticed how one strawberry doesn't taste like the next one, even from the same patch or box. No two tomatoes taste alike. You notice this when using organic produce which is more flavorful and also as your taste buds become more refined, which occurs from eating raw. Generally with cooked foods, many of the ingredients are processed, often containing chemical substances and bleached out ingredients such as flour and sugar, and always taste the same. Also with cooking, much of the flavor is cooked out & is often reintroduced with flavorings, which are again often chemical substances. When using fresh organic produce, there is always some flavor variance in the produce itself. Other factors which will affect flavor and significantly benefit a dish are how fresh and ripe the produce is. Generally the riper and fresher the produce, the more flavor there is, they become sweeter and more nutrients become available.

Glass Jars – are always preferable to store ingredients or leftover dishes and condiments in than plastic. While there are many different grades of plastic, some better than others, glass is the safest. It doesn't leach any chemicals or absorb any flavors from the foods. It is also easier to get completely clean and looks nicer. You and your food are worth it.

5 MEASUREMENT ABBREVIATIONS AND CONVERSIONS

t = teaspoon
T = tablespoon
c = cup
3 t = 1 T
4 T = ¼ c
1 cup = 8 ounces
1 quart = .95 liters
4 c = 1 quart
4 quarts = 1 gallon

Robin Gregory

6 RECIPES

DRINKS AND SMOOTHIES

Almond Milk

I always have a pitcher of almond milk in my fridge. I make it fresh about every 4 days. It is super easy to make, costs less than buying it premade at the store and tastes much better. This is the one item that I always seem to miss the most whenever I am traveling. Try making it yourself and see. I bet you will fall in love with it too!

2 c **Almonds** - presoaked
6 c **Water**

Blend well in blender and then strain in mesh nut milk bag. That's all there is to it. I usually use the pulp to make cookies with. The almond milk will keep in the fridge for 4 to 5 days. The left over almond pulp will keep for 6 to 7 days. It can be dehydrated or frozen for later use.

Vanilla Nut Milk

Vanilla Nut Milk is a delicious non-dairy base for some of my favorite smoothies. It is also great on breakfast cereals, in chai tea and just to drink on its own.

1 c **Almonds**
3 c **Water**
5 **Honey Dates**
1 t **Vanilla**

Blend well in blender. Strain in mesh nut milk bag. The leftover almond pulp can be used to make cookies. Milk will keep in the fridge for 3 days. Pulp will keep for 1 to 2 days longer. It can also be frozen for later use.

Almonds can be substituted with other nuts, such as: Brazil, cashew, hazelnut or pecan. Experiment with new flavors. Brazil nuts are a favorite of mine as well. Milk can also be made out of seeds and grains, such as: hemp, sesame and quinoa. Creating new recipes with raw foods is easy, fun and nourishing.

Chocolate Nut Milk

Chocolate milk – the raw healthy way!

1 ½ c *Vanilla Nut Milk*
1 T **Cacao Powder**

Blend and serve.

Strawberry Nut Milk

A quick trip back to childhood: sweet and delicious!

1 ½ c *Vanilla Nut Milk*
6 **Strawberries**

Blend and serve. Strawberries can be substituted for other berries or fruits – it's fun to experiment.

Banana Cardamom Milk

A thick rich milk with an exotic twist.

1 ½ c *Vanilla Nut Milk*
1 **Banana**
¼ t ground **Cardamom**

Blend and serve. Frozen bananas are slightly less nutritious, but they blend into a creamier drink.

Coconut Milk

Coconut Milk can substitute for *Almond Milk* or *Vanilla Nut Milk* in many recipes.

1 c **Coconut** meat from a mature brown coconut, peeled
2 c **Water**
1 t **Vanilla** – optional
1 **Medjool Date** or 3 to 4 Honey Dates – optional

Blend all ingredients together in a high speed blender and strain in a nut milk bag or cheesecloth. Pulp can be used to make cookies. Milk and pulp will keep well in the fridge for 3 to 4 days.

Tropical Green Smoothie

If I could only have one smoothie every day for the rest of my life, this would be it. The blended greens give you incredible nutrition but you really only taste the fruit. These are very delicious and sometimes I think I could live on just these.

1 c packed **Spinach**
1 **Kale** leaf
1 **Banana**
½ **Mango** - peeled and cubed, or ½ c if using frozen
1 c **Pineapple** - peeled and cubed
1 c **Water**

Put all ingredients in a blender and blend. A frozen banana will make it nice and creamy.

Berry Green Smoothie

Berries and Greens = Intense Nutrition and Delicious Flavor = Happiness and a Beautiful Life. Whoever thought nutrition could taste this good and be this easy!

¼ bunch **Spinach**, to equal 1 c packed
1 **Kale** leaf
1 **Banana**
½ **Apple** or Pear
½ c Mixed **Berries**
1 c **Water**

Place all ingredients in Blender and blend well. Enjoy often

Fruit Sensation Smoothie

This smoothie turns a beautiful peach pink color. It is one of the favorites with children. It is also an easy recipe to adapt depending on fruit available and in season.

1 **Banana**
½ **Orange**
½ **Apple**
½ c **Pineapple**
5 **Strawberries**
½ c **Water**

Peel banana and orange. Add all of the fruit into the blender and blend. You will need to add more water, up to one cup, if using frozen fruit, as it may be necessary to blend. Experiment with varying the quantities of fruit or substituting different fruits such as peaches, mangoes or different berries. It's easy to use this as a guide and come up with lots of your own flavor creations.

Strawberry Peach Smoothie

Sweet berry deliciousness!

12 **Strawberries**
1 c **Grapes**
2 **Peaches**
Water as necessary to blend.

Put the more watery fruit (in this recipe that's grapes) near the bottom of the blender, so that the blades will catch them first and you will have to add less additional water. Blend well and enjoy. This smoothie can be made green also - try adding 1 cup spinach.

Raspberry Beret Smoothie

Whimsical and delicious with an incredibly beautiful deep pink color!

1 **Banana**
½ **Orange**
½ c **Raspberries**
½ c **Water**

Add all ingredients to the blender and blend, add another half cup water, or as much as is necessary to blend smoothly if using frozen fruit.

ChocoMonkey Smoothie

This is for wild little chocolate-crazy monkeys. The ChocoMonkey is ultra-smooth and creamy chocolate goodness at its best!

1 c *Vanilla Nut Milk* or *Almond Milk*
1 **Banana**
1 T **Cacao powder**
1 T **Almond Butter**
1 **Medjool Date**
½ t **Cinnamon**
½ t **Vanilla**
Handful of ice cubes

Pit date and then add all ingredients in the blender and blend until creamy and smooth. My favorite add-on to this is a teaspoon of **Maca**, which creates a super-wild, super loveable chocolate monkey!

Tropical Beach Smoothie

Its palm trees, blue sky and sunshine anytime!

1 c *Coconut Milk*
1 **Banana**
½ **Mango**
1 **Orange**
1/8 **Pineapple**

Blend well, pour in a glass, sit back, get comfortable and let the visions come.

Protein Smoothie

This drink is loaded with protein and grounding. The hemp seeds are filling and give you energy for a long period of time. You can experiment with adding other fruits. Get creative and have fun. You can even take it further by adding some greens for even more protein and nutrition!

1c **Vanilla Nut Milk** or *Coconut Milk*
1 **Banana**
1 scoop **Hemp Protein**
½ c **Blueberries** or other Berries

Blend well & Enjoy!

Masala Chai

Masala Chai means literally 'mixed spice tea' and is made by brewing black tea with aromatic Indian spices and herbs. This is my favorite tea. It is well worth the effort to make it yourself and quite easy once you get used to it. It's a great tea to serve to guests and makes your kitchen smell amazing!

6 c **Water**
3 to 4 **Cinnamon** sticks
4 to 6 **Cloves**
1" **Ginger** – sliced
1 T **Cardamom** seeds
½ T **Fennel** seeds
2 **Black Tea bags**

Boil water and let sit for a few minutes to cool slightly. Crack open the cardamom pods slightly on a cutting board with the flat side of a chef's knife to open and reveal the delicious black seeds inside. Add these and rest of spices to tea pot and pour hot water over and let steep for at least 20 minutes. Add tea bags and let steep another 5 minutes. Strain spices and bags from tea. Serve tea with *Vanilla Nut Milk* or *Almond Milk* and agave or sweetener of choice if desired.

Sesame Milk Tea

This is an easy to make healthy creamy comfort tea.

1 T **Tahini**
3 **Honey Dates**
½ t **Vanilla**
¼ t **Cinnamon**
2 c **Hot Water**

Blend all together in blender. Pour into a big mug and Enjoy!

BREAKFASTS

Apple Cinnamon Oatmeal

This was one of my favorite early recipes which helped me get through my first winter raw. The Canadian winter can be a real test and this cereal, on those cold January mornings, helps a lot.

Note: The winters after your first one detoxing are much easier to get through and they keep getting easier. But this cereal is still a treat, as well as warming and very hearty.

1 c steel-cut **Oat groats**
4 **Apples**
¼ c **Almonds** and/or **Walnuts**, chopped
¼ c **Raisins** and/or **Goji berries**
1 t **Cinnamon**
1 Tbsp **Maple Syrup** or Agave

Place oats in bowl. If steel-cut oats are hard to find, pulse chop whole oat groats until coarse in coffee grinder or processor. Peel and core apples and grind through a juicer with the blank screen or in food processor. Mix apples and rest of ingredients with the oats. Mixture should be fairly wet, if not add a bit of water. Cover and let mixture sit together a few hours before eating or make it the night before so it will be ready for breakfast. Refrigerate, if you will be letting it sit over 12 hours before eating.

Fruit, Nut and Seed Bowl

This is a really easy and delicious morning cereal to put together. Just put in a bowl the nuts, seeds and fruit that you have readily available.

Mix chopped **Peaches**, **Pears**, **Kiwi**, **Berries** or fruits of choice together in a bowl.
Add a variety of chopped nuts and seeds such as: **Almonds**, **Pecans**, **Walnuts**, **Cashews**, **Hazelnuts**, **Pine nuts**, **Pumpkin seeds** and/or **Hemp seeds**.
Add some dried fruit to mixture, such as: **Raisins**, **Currants**, **Cranberries**, **Cherries** or **Goji berries**
Pour *Vanilla Nut Milk* or *Almond Milk* over the mixture and then drizzle some **Agave** or **Maple Syrup** on top, if desired.
Enjoy!

Option: Instead of *Almond Milk*, blend or mash a banana with ½ cup of water until creamy and pour on top. Add a dash of vanilla and cinnamon to mixture if desired.

Blueberry Pancakes

These make a wonderful breakfast and a great snack. Kids love them!

1 c **Walnuts**
1 c **Cashews**
1 c **Blueberries**
½ c **Agave**
½ c **Water -** or more, as needed for desired consistency
1 t **Vanilla**
½ t **Cinnamon**

Soak nuts for 1 to 2 hours. Then process them until smooth in food processor with the water, vanilla and cinnamon. Pancake batter should be thin enough to spread easily and yet thick enough that it holds its shape when spread out into circles. Add ¼ cup of water and then gradually add more water while processing to reach correct consistency. Then transfer this mixture to a bowl and add the blueberries. If they are frozen, mix them in quickly just before spreading out so the batter doesn't turn purple from over mixing. You could also sprinkle on top of formed pancakes and press them into the batter. Spread batter by just under ¼ cup spoonfuls to make 8 to 4" circles. Dehydrate at 115 degrees for 3 to 4 hours. Flip and continue dehydrating overnight so pancakes are warm and ready to eat in the morning.

Buckwheaties

This delicious cereal will keep well for a long time, up to a month or longer, and it is easy to make so make lots. Buckwheaties are great topped with additional fruit and served with *Vanilla Nut Milk* or *Almond Milk* and a little sweetener of choice.

6 c **Buckwheat** – sprouted
1 c dried shredded **Coconut**
1 c **Pecans**
1 **Apple**
1 T **Cinnamon**

Finely chop the pecans and apple in a food processor. Blend with buckwheat, coconut and cinnamon in a bowl. Spread on teflex sheets and dehydrate overnight at 115 degrees, until very dry and crispy. Break into pieces and store in a container in the refrigerator. This will keep well for a few weeks.

Sprouting Buckwheat

For each cup you need sprouted, use 2/3 cup of seed.
Soak Buckwheat for 30 to 60 minutes in a bowl.
After this time pour the Buckwheat into a large metal colander and rinse. The water will be very murky. Keep rinsing, a lot!, until the water runs clear.
Let sit for another 4 to 8 hours and rinse well again.
Let sit for another 4 to 8 hours and rinse well again.
Let sit for another 4 to 8 hours and rinse well again.
Continue this until you have little tails emerging, this tile after you rinse them let them sit for 8 to 12 hours until quite dry. They will store better dry. However, they do not store well for a long time, so try to only make as many as you plan to use right away.

Granola

This is a wonderful and delicious granola recipe! The recipe makes lots but if you have a large dehydrator you may wish to double the recipe. It is guaranteed to get eaten quickly.

1 c **Almonds**
1 c **Walnuts**
2 c **Pecans**
1 c **Sunflower seeds**
2 **Apples**
1 **Banana**
½ c **Raisins**

Sauce:
1 c **Dates**
1/3 c **Water**
½ c **Maple Syrup**
1 t **Vanilla**
1 t **Salt**

Blend sauce ingredients in blender and set aside. Process the nuts and sunflower seeds in food processor until they are in small pieces. Remove to a large bowl. Process apples, banana and raisins together until coarsely chopped and chunky and add to bowl. Add the ground flax and sauce to the rest of granola ingredients in bowl and mix together until well combined.

Spread out onto teflex sheets approximately ¼" thick. Dehydrate 4 to 6 hours at 115 degrees, then flip onto mesh screen and continue dehydrating for 10 to 12 hours. Break into pieces and store in an air-tight container. This will keep well for several weeks. To keep fresh for longer, store the granola in the refrigerator.

Granola Variations

Forest Burst Granola – Add ½ c dried **Cranberries** and 2 T **Cinnamon**

Hola Granola – Add ½ chopped **Pineapple** and ½ c shredded **Coconut**

Deluxe Granola – Add ½ c **Coconut**, ½ c **Cranberries**, ½ c **Pineapple**, 1 T **Cinnamon** and 1 T **Orange zest**

APPETIZERS

Spring Rolls

These are truly delicious and are great to make when entertaining or for a group of people. The vegetable filling mixture can be made and stored in the fridge for several days, so they can be rolled and eaten whenever desired.

10 to 12 **Rice paper wrappers** or Collard or soft Lettuce leaves
2 c **Zucchini** – grated
2 c **Carrots** – grated
1 c **Purple Cabbage** – sliced finely
½ **Red Pepper**
2 **Green Onions** – finely sliced
1" **Ginger** – minced or grated
10 **Mint leaves** – chopped
¼ c **Basil leaves** – chopped
¼ c **Cilantro leaves** – chopped
1 T **Sesame Oil**
1 T **Olive Oil**
1 t **Salt**

Mix all ingredients except the rice paper wrappers together in a big bowl. To soften rice paper wrapper: place the rice paper under warm water for 5 seconds until it starts to soften. Lay flat and place ¼ cup of vegetable mixture in middle but closer to the bottom, fold up bottom of wrapper around it, roll up a little, then fold in sides and roll up tightly. For collards cut into a 6"x 6" square and roll the same way. Serve with nama shoyu or *Tamarind Dipping Sauce*.
The recipe makes approximately 24 rolls.

Tamarind Dipping Sauce

This distinctively flavored dipping sauce is so delicious and great served with freshly made spring rolls. This sauce is a definite favorite.

1 c **Tamarind Paste**
½ c **Agave**
2 T **Nama Shoyu**
2 T **Olive Oil**
1" **Ginger** - minced
1 t **Salt**
½ t **Caraway**
½ t ground **Coriander seed**
Dash of **Anise** and **Garlic powder**

To make the tamarind paste - see instructions under Tamarind listing in Ingredients section. This is the longest part, after this is finished blend it with the rest of the ingredients together in a blender. This sauce will keep in the fridge for 2 to 3 weeks.

Spicy Shoyu Dipping Sauce

This very easy to make and delicious dipping sauce is very spicy but you can add less chili if you prefer.

¼ c **Nama Shoyu**
2 T **Olive Oil**
1 T **Agave**
1 t **Sambal Oelek,** or ground Chili Pepper or Cayenne

Blend all ingredients together well. This sauce will keep in the fridge for up to a month.

Nori Rolls

These maki nori rolls are made with sprouted quinoa, which is easy to make with the following directions. Quinoa can be substituted with a bed of alfalfa or broccoli sprouts. Layer with lots of colorful vegetables and roll up, slice and Voila! They are beautiful as well as delicious.

Nori Sheets
Sunflower Spread
Sprouted Quinoa
Sprouts: Alfalfa, Broccoli or Sunflower
Vegetables: Carrot, Red Pepper, Cucumber, Avocado, Green Onion and/or Daikon Radish. - julienned into long thin strips or grated optional – *Marinated Shitake Mushrooms*

Lay a nori sheet on a bamboo sushi roller mat, if available. On the nori sheet spread on the half closest to you a strip of *Sunflower Pate*. On top of the pate, spread a layer of *Sprouted Quinoa* and then layer with desired sprouts and vegetables. Drizzle lightly with a dipping sauce or nama shoyu and cayenne, if desired. Roll up tightly using the mat to help press the roll together. If a mat is not available just roll it up as tightly as possible. Wet the end as you reach it with a bit of water or nama shoyu to seal. Press together after it is rolled for a few seconds to make sure the roll is tightly sealed. Release and cut into 6 pieces – cutting in half and then each half into thirds. Serve with nama shoyu or *Spicy Shoyu Dipping Sauce*.

Sprouting Quinoa

Soak quinoa in water to cover for at least a half hour. Drain and rinse quinoa in a fine mesh strainer. After it has drained set the strainer with the quinoa still in it in a bowl. Let it sit there for several hours where air can circulate freely around it. It is best left at room temperature and out of direct sunlight. Rinse and drain again in 8 to 12 hours. Again leave quinoa in strainer sitting in bowl. Repeat, rinsing and draining one more time, in 8 to 12 hours. Quinoa sprouts can be used now and for up to 24 hours. If using later, store in the refrigerator. They will be quite small but taste great when they are very young sprouts and are best used as soon as possible for freshest taste.

Marinated Shitake Mushrooms

These mushrooms are so delicious after being marinated that there have been times when they have not even lasted to go into the recipe that called for them. They are delicious in nori rolls and also on sandwiches, pizza, salads and just by themselves.

2 c **Shitake Mushrooms** - sliced
2 T **Olive Oil**
1 T **Nama Shoyu**
1 **Garlic** clove - minced
½ t **Cardamom**
½ t **Cumin**
¼ t **Black pepper**
dash **Cayenne**

Mix the marinade and then add the sliced mushrooms to it and allow to sit stirring occasionally for 20 minutes to several hours. These will keep for several days in the fridge.

Dolmas

This classic Mediterranean dish, also known as stuffed grape leaves, gets transformed into a living cuisine recreation with parsnip rice. The grape leaves can be purchased at most larger supermarkets and usually enough come in a bottle to make this recipe many times.

1 c **Parsnip**
1 **Tomato** – diced small
1 small **Onion** – diced small
½ **Red Pepper** – diced small
¼ c **Currants**
2 T **Olive Oil**
½ **Lemon** - juiced
2 **Garlic** cloves – minced
2 t **Oregano**
1 t **Cinnamon**
Grape leaves – soaked in filtered water, rinsed and patted dry.

Grape leaves come bottled in a brine liquid. One bottle will be more than enough. Soak, rinse and dry leaves while you prepare rice mixture. Process the parsnips into rice size pieces in a food processor. Mix the parsnip rice with the rest of the ingredients except for the grape leaves, in a bowl, combining well. Spoon one to two tablespoons of the mixture into a grape leaf, vein side up. Roll it up like a burrito, folding the bottom up over the stuffing and then folding the side leaves in toward the center. Then roll up until you have a little cigar shaped packet. The mixture should be fully enclosed.

SOUPS

Creamy Miso Noodle Soup

This is one of my favorite foods; sometimes I think I could live on this soup alone.

1 pkg. **Kelp Noodles** or 2 c Zucchini – spiralized into noodles and chopped
2 c *Almond Milk,* or 2 T Almond Butter and 2 c water
3 T **White Miso**
1 t **Nama Shoyu**
1 t **Agave**
1 t **Sesame Oil**
1 t **Sambal Oelek**, or 1 t fresh Chili
½" **Ginger** – chopped
1 **Garlic** clove – chopped
Cayenne to taste
3 c **Water**
2 **Green Onions** – thinly sliced diagonally
2 T **Red Pepper** – finely chopped

Soften kelp noodles by soaking in hot water (up to 115 degrees) overnight or for several hours. Blend all ingredients except noodles, green onions and red pepper in a blender. Rinse kelp noodles well and drain. Place noodles, red pepper and green onion into warm soup broth and let sit at a warm temperature to continue to soften noodles and also the green onion and pepper for 20 to 30 minutes. Serve warm.

Butternut Squash Soup

This creamy soup has a delicate sweet and spicy flavor that is quite enticing, and it is incredibly easy to make, just blend it all together!

3 c **Butternut Squash** – peeled and cubed
1 **Apple** – peeled, cored and cubed
1 **Avocado**
1 T **Nama Shoyu**
2 T **Olive Oil**
½" **Ginger** - minced
1 t **Salt**
½ t **Cumin**
¼ t **Onion powder**
¼ t **Cinnamon**
1 to 1 ½ c **Water**, as necessary to reach desired consistency

Blend all ingredients except avocado together in blender. After well pureed, blend in the avocado to make creamy smooth. This soup can be served cold or warm. It will keep for 2 days in the refrigerator

Creamy Tomato Thai Soup

I love this soup. It is really delicious and another of my favorites!

3 large **Tomatoes** - quartered
1 **Red Pepper** - quartered
¼ **Onion** - chopped
1 **Jalapeno** - chopped
1 **Garlic** clove - chopped
¾" **Ginger** - minced
½ c **Young Thai Coconut meat** & ½ c **water**, or 1 c Coconut milk
2 T **Lemon juice**
1 **Avocado**
1 T **Nama Shoyu**
2 T **Agave**
2 T **Olive Oil**
4 **Basil** leaves
Dash each of: **Salt, Black pepper, Cayenne** and **Cumin**
Water - as needed for desired consistency

Blend all together ingredients except avocado, oil and water together in blender. When well pureed add avocado and stream pour in oil slowly to make creamy. Add water if necessary to reach desired consistency. Adjust seasonings to taste. This soup will keep for 2 days refrigerated.

Green Goddess Spinach Herb Soup

Green Soups are a wonderful way to get lots of greens. Try experimenting with different herbs. This tastes great with a little fresh dill, try adding a teaspoon for flavor. Delicious!

4 c **Spinach**
½ **Apple**
1 **Avocado**
½ c fresh **Herbs**: Basil, Cilantro, Oregano, Parsley, Rosemary, Thyme
½ T **Nama Shoyu**
½ **Lemon** – juiced

1 T **Agave**
1 **Garlic** clove
Dashes of **Salt, Black pepper** and **Cayenne** to taste
1 c **Water**

Puree all ingredients, except the avocado, in a blender. When smooth add the avocado and blend until smooth and creamy. Add more water if necessary to reach desired soup consistency. This soup will keep well for 2 days refrigerated.

Gazpacho

This is a delicious summer recipe. The balsamic vinegar is not raw and optional but a very small amount adds a lot of flavor.

2 large **Tomatoes** - chop 1 of the tomatoes and set aside
1 **Red Pepper** - chop half and set aside
1 **Cucumber** - chop one quarter and set aside
2 **Green Onions** - finely slice one green onion and set aside
1 **Garlic** clove
3 T **Olive Oil**
½ **Lemon** – juiced
1 t **Balsamic Vinegar** - omit to have this soup be completely raw
1 T fresh **Basil** – half chopped and set aside
1 T fresh **Oregano** – half chopped and set aside
½ t **Salt**
Dash of **Cumin, Cayenne**

Blend all of the ingredients together, except for one tomato, half of the red pepper, a quarter of the cucumber, one green onion and half of the chopped fresh herbs, which have been chopped and set aside. Transfer the blended mixture to a bowl and mix in the reserved chopped vegetables and herbs. Stir well and let sit for an hour before serving, to give it time for flavors to marry. Will keep for 3 to 4 days refrigerated.

Carrot Ginger Soup

This slightly spicy, sweet and creamy soup is rich, yet light and distinctively delicious.

4 c **Carrots** – pureed through juicer with blank plate
1 **Avocado**
½ **Lemon** – juiced
1 T **Agave**
1 T **Olive Oil**
1 T **Cilantro leaves** - chopped
1" **Ginger** – chopped
½ t **Salt**
dash of **Black pepper** and **Cayenne** to taste

Blend all ingredients except avocado, olive oil and cilantro in a blender. Add the avocado and blend again, and while blending stream in the olive oil. After well blended stir in cilantro leaves and serve. This soup will keep for 2 days refrigerated.

MAIN DISHES

Pizza

This is a favorite recipe. It consists of a special *Veggie-Seed Pizza Crust* topped with *Garlic Ginger Almond Cheese,* or *Cashew Cheese,* and *Pizza Sauce.* It can be loaded with a variety of toppings, or eaten just as a cheese pizza. It is extra delicious sprinkled with *Pine Nut Parmesan* on top. Mmm.. everyone loves Pizza!

Garlic Ginger Almond Cheese

This almond cheese had an incredible flavor: sweet, salty and lightly spicy. It is nothing like dairy cheese, a whole different entity, but one worth getting to know. The miso is what is used to lightly ferment the almonds and create the good bacteria, the friendly flora so beneficial to our digestive system and body.

2 c **Almonds**
2 T **Miso**
2 c **Water**
3 T **Olive Oil**
2 **Garlic** cloves - minced
1" **Ginger** – minced or grated
1 t **Salt**
½ t **Onion powder**
¼ t **Chili powder**
¼ t **Cayenne**

Process the almonds in a food processor or blender until coarsely chopped. Add miso and 2 cups of water to the processor and continue processing until it is well mixed and a coarse-fine texture. Transfer the mixture to a sterilized glass bottle or bowl and cover with a mesh screen or cheesecloth and elastic, so that the mixture can breathe. Set in a warm place and allow the cheese to ferment for 10 to 12 hours. At this time it will likely have separated and may have little bubbles in it. If not, it may not have been warm enough but it will still taste great. Continue and strain the whey, the liquid part, from the cheese in a mesh nut bag or in cheesecloth. Let drain and gently squeeze out the liquid then transfer to the food processor.

Combine the almond cheese with oil and spices in a food processor and process until well combined. Add water, if necessary, for mixture to be wet enough to fold over while processing. Almond cheese will keep well in the refrigerator for up to 2 weeks.

Cashew Cheese

This mild, delicious and easy to make cashew cheese is ready to use right away.

2 c **Cashews** – soaked 2-4 hours
2 T **Nutritional Yeast**
1 T **Lemon juice**
1 t **Salt**

Drain the cashews and process them in a food processor with the rest of ingredients until creamy and smooth. This cheese can be stored in a covered container in the refrigerator for a week.

Pizza Sauce

Raw tomato sauces are easily as good as cooked! This one is rich and thick and best made with fresh herbs when available.

1 c **Sun-dried Tomatoes**
2 **Tomatoes**
¼ **Red Pepper**
2 T **Onion**
1 **Garlic** clove
4 large **Basil** leaves, or 1t dried
1½ t **Oregano**
1 t **Salt**
½ t **Marjoram**
½ t **Thyme**
½ t **Cayenne**, or to taste

Blend all ingredients together in blender or puree in food processor.

Pizza Topping Ideas

Marinated Shitakes, Red Pepper and Green Onion

Black Olive, Red Pepper, Pineapple and Red Onion

Marinated Fennel and Onion with slivered Carrots and Hot Banana Peppers

---

Marinated Fennel and Onion

This is a delicious topping that goes with many other dishes. These are great to put in raw sandwiches as well as on salads. This can be used as a condiment on the side of your plate or served with your meal. Always have a glass bottle of these on hand in the fridge.

1 c **Fennel** – finely sliced
1 c **Sweet Onion** – finely sliced

Marinade:
½ c **Apple Cider Vinegar**
¼ c **Honey**
2 T **Nama Shoyu**
2 **Garlic** cloves – minced

Mix marinade in a glass bottle. Add the fennel and onion to the mixture in the bottle, screw cap on well and shake to mix and cover thoroughly. Other vegetables such as hot or sweet peppers, carrots etc. can also be marinated this way. Let vegetables marinate a few hours before using.

This mixture will keep well in the fridge for several weeks. You can continue to add vegetables to marinade as they are used. However, completely replace the marinade and vegetable mixture in a clean bottle at least once a month.

Pine Nut Parmesan

This is a wonderful Parmesan alternative that tastes great. It's so easy to switch over to this one!

It also is good without dehydrating and even easier to make.

1 c **Pine nuts**
1 T **Nutritional Yeast**
1 t **Salt**

Process all ingredients together in a food processor. Transfer and spread out onto teflex sheets and dehydrate several hours until dry. Store parmesan in an air tight container or glass jar.

Zucchetti Pasta Dishes

In raw cuisine zucchini is transformed into pasta usually and simply by using a vegetable spiralizer (see Equipment). Any solid firm vegetable can be spiralized and used. Root vegetables such as carrots and sweet potatoes work very well. Experiment with lots of different vegetables such as cucumbers, daikon radishes, squash.

If you do not have access to a spiralizer you can easily make linguini pasta with a vegetable slicer. Simply peel the outer skin of the zucchini, throw away this part (or save for juicing) and continue peeling long strips using the vegetable peeler. Voila, zucchini linguini!

When pasta is made, place in a bowl and top with sauce, or if preferred, toss together with sauce first and then place in bowl to serve. Pasta dishes are extra delicious topped with *Pine Nut Parmesan*.

Tomato Marinara Sauce

This is a wonderful tomato sauce. Thick and rich and delicious!

3 to 4 **Tomatoes** - chopped in large pieces
½ c **Sun-dried Tomatoes** - soaked
½ **Red Pepper** - chopped in large pieces
¼ **Onion** - chopped in large pieces
1 **Jalapeno**
1 T **Olive Oil**
1 **Garlic** clove
1 T **Agave**
1 T **Apple Cider Vinegar**
1 T each of fresh **Oregano** and **Basil**, or use 1 to 2 t dried
1 t **Salt**
Dash **Cayenne** - to taste

Blend the sun-dried tomatoes with a little of the soak water and all of the ingredients except 2 of the tomatoes, the red pepper and onions in the blender and puree. Keep the rest of the soak water from sun dried tomatoes aside in case you need a little more to achieve the desired consistency. Process the tomatoes, red pepper and onion in a food processor until they are chunky-fine texture and mix all of the ingredients together. Sauce will keep for 1 to 2 weeks refrigerated. Serve over spiralized zucchini noodles.

Alfredo Sauce

Smooth, silky, subtle and rich. This raw vegan version of the classic is delicious on its own and also adds an extra richness when added to any of the other pasta sauces or layered in a wrap. This is a diversified sauce which is great to have on hand and delicious to use in many dishes from spreading on sandwiches to adding to sauces or salad dressings to make them rich and creamy.

1 c **Cashews** – soaked 1 to 2 hours and drained
1 c **Pine nuts**
½ c **Olive Oil**
½ **Lemon** – juiced
2 **Garlic** cloves
½ t **Black pepper**
½ t **Salt**
¼ t **Nutmeg**
½ to 1 c **Water**

Blend altogether in a blender. Add just enough water to make into a creamy smooth, easy to pour and yet thick consistency. Sauce will keep for 1 to 2 weeks refrigerated.

Basil Spinach Pesto

This delicious, rich and flavorful pesto sauce is so easy to make. For even more flavor, when in season use more basil in this recipe. If you grow lots of basil in a garden in the summer, or can obtain big bunches of it, often available at farmers markets in season, the leaves can be washed, dried and then processed with olive oil in a food processor. This mixture can then be frozen in ice cube trays and stored in zip-lock bags in the freezer. The smell when using this basil in the winter is like bringing summer back into your kitchen.

1 bunch **Spinach**, to equal 4 c packed leaves
1 large bunch **Basil**, to equal 1 c packed leaves
1 c **Pine nuts**
1 c **Walnuts** or Sunflower seeds - soaked 2 to 4 hours

¼ c **Olive Oil**
½ **Lemon** – juiced
3 **Garlic** cloves
¼ t **Salt**

Wash and measure spinach and basil leaves. Rinse and drain walnuts or sunflower seeds. Process all ingredients together in food processor. Serve over zucchini pasta. Pesto will keep for 1 to 2 weeks refrigerated.

Olive Coconut Curry Sauce

The delightful and unique flavor combination of this dish comes together into a deliciously rich taste sensation that can be addictive!

3 **Tomatoes** - diced
8 **Black Olives** – pitted and diced fine
2 T **Coconut Cream** or ¼ c Coconut meat and 1 T Coconut oil
1 T **Olive Oil**
½ **Lemon** – juiced, to equal 2 T
1 t **Basil** and **Oregano**
1 t **Curry**
1 t **Salt**
¼ t **Cumin**
¼ t **Turmeric**
dash of **Cayenne**

Chop 2 of the tomatoes and set these with the olives aside in a bowl. Process all of the rest of the ingredients. Pour over tomato & olives in a bowl and mix together. Serve over spiralized zucchini or vegetable pasta. Sauce will keep for 2 to 3 days refrigerated but is best made and served fresh.

Lasagna

4 **Zucchinis** – peel and cut into long, flat strips with a vegetable peeler
4 **Tomatoes** - sliced thin
1 recipe of *Tomato Marinara Sauce*
1 recipe of *Basil Spinach Pesto*
1 recipe of *Cashew Cheese*

In a rectangular, 9"x 13" or larger, baking pan or glass or ceramic dish place a layer of zucchini strips on the bottom of the pan, overlapping them some to make a flat base covering the bottom.
Next spread a layer of marinara sauce covering the zucchini 'noodles'. Then place spoonfuls of cashew cheese and pesto on top of the marinara layer. Top with tomato slices.

Repeat these steps again 2 more times, placing 2 more layers of zucchini strips, marinara, cashew cheese, pesto and tomatoes, so that there are 3 layers of each. The last layer is finished off with tomato slices on top.

Wraps

Collard leaves make a perfect alternative to wrap around tasty fillings for the perfect lunch. Wraps can also be made with other lettuce leaves such as romaine and the large outer iceberg leaves. Although iceberg is almost devoid of any nutrients, the crunch is nice. However, I think that collard leaves really make the best wraps, and many skeptics have been converted from their very first bite. Try some of these wonderfully nutritious and delicious combinations.

Nut Loaf Patty Wraps – In a collard leaf layer *Basil Spinach Pesto*, a *Nut Loaf Patty*, Tomato slices, Red Onion, shredded Lettuce, and *Pine-nut Sauce.* Fold bottom of leaf up and then fold each side in and around the filling.

Taco Wraps – In a collard leaf layer *Ginger Garlic Almond Cheese*, a *Nut Loaf Patty*, *Guacamole*, chopped Tomatoes, Red Onion, shredded Lettuce and *Salsa*. Fold bottom of leaf up and then fold each side in and around the filling.

Nut Loaf Patties

These flavorful dehydrated patties are made from nuts, seeds, fresh vegetables, herbs and Portobello mushrooms which give a wonderful meaty texture. They make a perfect filling for wraps. Just add your favorite toppings and condiments and enjoy. Nut loaf patties are great eaten alone and make a perfect side to a big salad.

1 c **Walnuts** - soaked, rinsed and drained
1 c **Almonds** – soaked, rinsed and drained
½ c **Sunflower seeds** - soaked, rinsed and drained
½ c **Pumpkin seeds** - soaked, rinsed and drained
1 c **Portobello Mushrooms** – chopped
1 **Red Pepper** – finely chopped
½ c **Sun-dried Tomatoes** - finely chopped
½ c **Cilantro** or **Parsley** – chopped
1 **Red Onion**, approximately 1 c – chopped
¼ c **Olive Oil**
2 T **Nama Shoyu**
2 **Garlic** cloves – chopped
2 t **Salt**
1 t each **Cumin, Chili powder, Onion powder** and **Oregano**
½ t **Cayenne**

Process together nuts and seeds until coarsely chopped in food processor and then transfer to a bowl. Add the rest of the ingredients and mix well together. Form into patties and dehydrate on teflex sheets at 115 degrees for 4 to 6 hours. Flip onto a mesh screen and continue dehydrating for an additional 6 to 8 hours until fairly dry. These patties keep well stored in an air tight container in the fridge for 1 to 2 weeks.

Pine Nut Sauce

A decadently delicious creamy sauce that is wonderful added to wraps and to drizzle on pasta dishes and nut loaf patties with. A bonus is how easy this sauce is to make.

1 c **Pine nuts**
½ **Lemon** – juiced
Salt and **Pepper,** to taste

Blend together in blender to make smooth and creamy sauce with just as much water as necessary to make it just thick enough to be able to pour, slowly.
Pine nut sauce will keep for 1 week in the fridge.

Pad Thai

This raw version is close to the authentic and very popular Thai dish, made with tamarind and with all of the distinctive flavors of the original. It excites all of the taste buds at once as you experience all of the flavor sensations; sweet, sour, salty, tangy and spicy. It is very satisfying!

1 pkg. **Kelp Noodles** – soaked in as hot water as possible to stay raw (under115 degrees), for several hours to soften.
1 **Green Zucchini** – spiralized
1 **Yellow Zucchini** – spiralized
1 **Carrot** – angel hair spiralized
½ **Red Pepper** – julienned
6 to 8 leaves **Nappa Cabbage** – thinly sliced
¼ c **Cilantro leaves** – chopped

Sauce:
1 c **Cashews**
2 T **Almond Butter**
1 **Tomato**
¼ c **Tamarind Paste**
3 **Medjool Dates**
2 T **Nama Shoyu**
2 T **Olive Oil**
1 T **Sesame Oil**
1 **Lime** – juiced
1 **Garlic** clove
1 t **Salt**
½ t **Black pepper**
½ t **Sambal Oelek** or 1 t Chili – seeds removed
¼ t **Coriander seed**

Topping and Garnish:
¼ c **Cashews** – coarsely chopped
½ t **Sesame Oil**
½ t **Salt**
2 **Green Onions** – sliced diagonally
2 T **Red Pepper** – diced small

For the topping, mix chopped cashews with sesame oil and salt together in a small bowl and set aside until ready to serve.

Soak kelp noodles in 110 degree water overnight or for several hours to soften. Prepare the vegetables and set aside in a bowl. When the kelp noodles are soft, rinse and drain and then add to the bowl of vegetables.

Make the Pad Thai sauce by blending all of the sauce ingredients in a blender until smooth and creamy. To make the tamarind paste - see instructions under Tamarind listing in Ingredients section.

Mix sauce with vegetables and noodles until well combined. Serve in a bowl, garnished with Sesame cashews, green onion and red pepper.

DIPS AND PATES

Sprouted Chickpea Hummus

Hummus from sprouted chickpeas gives you more nutrition, more enzymes and a higher quality protein.

2 c sprouted **Chickpeas**
¼ c **Tahini**
¼ c **Olives** – pitted
¼ c **Cilantro leaves**
1 **Lime** – juiced
¼ c **Olive Oil**
3 **Garlic** cloves
1 **Jalapeno** or Chili or 1 t Sambal Oelek
1 t **Cumin**
1 t **Salt**
½ t **Onion powder**

Blend all ingredients together in a food processor until smooth. Hummus will keep well refrigerated for over one week.

Black Olive Tapenade

Black olive tapenade is a delicious spread on crackers. I love to layer dips for different taste sensations and this one adds incredible flavor. Also it is amazingly easy to make!

2 c **Kalamata Olives** – pitted and finely chopped
¼ c **Olive Oil**
½ **Lemon** – juiced
1 **Garlic** clove
1 T **Parsley**
½ t **Oregano**
½ t **Thyme**
½ t **Savory**
½ t **Black Pepper** – freshly ground
Cayenne to taste

Process all ingredients in food processor until smooth. Store the tapenade in an air tight container in the fridge. This will keep for 2 weeks.

Guacamole

This traditional Mexican dish is an ultimate raw food. Avocados can keep you going for a long time with their healthy fats and intense nutrition. There are many variations of guacamole; it starts with just avocado, lemon and garlic and then you add in from there.

2 **Avocados**
2 T **Lemon juice,** or Lime juice
1 **Garlic** clove- minced
½ t **Salt**
Dash **Cumin** and **Cayenne**

optional ingredients include:
1 **Tomato** – seeded and diced
2 T **Onion** – chopped fine
1 **Jalapeno**, or Serrano Chili – minced
2 T **Cilantro leaves** – chopped

Mash the avocado with a fork. Add citrus juice, garlic and seasonings and mix well. Add any optional ingredients you wish and blend again to mix. Serve immediately. Store covered.

Spinach Dip

This creamy vegetable dip makes a great spread on crackers.

1 bunch **Spinach**, approximately 4 to 6 c
2 **Zucchini**
1 **Lemon** – juiced
1 **Avocado**
1 **Garlic** clove
½" **Ginger**
½ t **Salt**
¼ t each: **Cumin**, **Chili powder** and **Onion powder**

Process all of the ingredients, except for the avocado, together in a food processor. After well blended, add the avocado and process well into mixture. This dip will keep for 3 to 4 days refrigerated.

Veggie Nut Pate

Pates are very versatile. This one is great to spread on crackers and also as a side, served with a big salad. Any leftovers can be formed into patties and dehydrated (for further instructions - follow directions for *Nut Loaf Patties*).

2 c **Almonds**
2 c **Carrots**
3 **Celery** – finely chopped
¼ c **Red Onion** – finely chopped
1 **Garlic** clove
¼ c mixed fresh **Herbs** – chopped, or 2 T dried
1 t **Salt**
½ t **Cumin**
1 t **Chili powder**

Puree the almonds and carrots through a juicer with a blank screen or process as finely as possible in a food processor. Mix well together with rest of ingredients in a bowl. The pate will keep refrigerated for up to a week. This can be eaten right away and any leftovers can be made into burgers.

To make burgers: shape into patties and dehydrate on teflex at 115 degrees for 4 to 6 hours. Flip onto mesh screen and continue for another 6 to 8 hours. These store well in the refrigerator for up to 2 weeks.

Sun-dried Tomato Sunflower Pate

This pate makes a great base; it can be spread on crackers, on bread, on pizza and also makes a great base for nori rolls.

2 c **Sunflower seeds** – soaked, rinsed and drained
½ c **Sun-dried Tomatoes** – soak in water to rehydrate and drain, save soak water
1 bunch **Green Onions**
½ bunch **Parsley**, approximately ½ c
3 T **Olive Oil**
2 T **Nama Shoyu**
1 t **Basil**
1 t **Paprika**
1 t **Salt**
½ t **Black Pepper**
dash of **Cayenne**

Process all ingredients together in a food processor until smooth. Add just enough of the tomato soak water for ingredients to blend. Store the pate in an air tight container in the fridge. It will keep well for a week.

Portobello Herb Pate

This savory nut pate makes a great spread on crackers.

1 c **Portobello Mushrooms** – chopped
2 T **Olive Oil**
2 T **Nama Shoyu**
1 c **Walnuts** – soaked
½ c **Sunflower seeds** – soaked
½ c **Almonds** – soaked
1 **Red Pepper**
½ **Onion**, approximately ½ c
½ c fresh **Herbs**, such as: Rosemary, Marjoram, Chives, Thyme, Sage or Basil
1 **Garlic** clove – chopped
½ t **Salt**
½ t **Pepper**
Cayenne to taste

Marinate Portobellos in olive oil and nama shoyu for an hour or while the rest of ingredients are prepared. Process nuts and seeds together well first, and then process all of the ingredients together in a food processor. Store the pate in an air tight container in the fridge. This will keep for a week.

Mango Chutney

This recipe is another favorite. Mango chutney makes a delicious accompaniment to savory dishes and is great spread on crackers.

1 **Mango**, approximately 1½ c – peeled, cored and chopped
¼ c **Red Pepper** – chopped
¼ c **Pineapple** - chopped
¼ c **Onion** – chopped
¼ c **Raisins**
¼ c **Agave**
½ T **Apple Cider Vinegar**
½" **Ginger** – minced
1 **Garlic** clove – minced
1 T **Cilantro leaves** - chopped
½ t **Garam Masala**
¼ t **Chili**
¼ t **Mustard powder**
¼ t **Salt**

dash of **Cayenne** to taste

Process all ingredients except mango, red pepper, pineapple and onion, together in a food processor. Add onion and pulse chop until coarsely chopped. Add red pepper and pineapple and repeat, pulse-chopping into mixture. Put chopped mangoes in a bowl and pour processed chutney mixture on top. Stir until well combined and let sit together, stirring occasionally, for at least an hour before serving. Store chutney in an air-tight container in the fridge. It will keep for 1 to 2 weeks in the fridge.

Salsa

This salsa is a delicious mildly spicy enzyme-intact raw version of the classic. For spicier salsa add more jalapeno or cayenne.

4 **Tomatoes**
½ **Onion**
½ **Red Pepper**
3 sprigs of **Cilantro** – finely chopped
2 T **Celery leaves** – chop down from top of stalks
1 **Garlic** clove
1 **Jalapeno**
1 T **Apple Cider Vinegar**, or fresh Lemon juice
1 t **Salt**
½ t **Chili**
½ t **Onion powder**
¼ t **Cumin**

Chop half of the tomatoes, onion and red pepper and put into a bowl with the cilantro. Put the other half of the vegetables and the rest of the ingredients in a food processor or blender and blend until fine. Add to the ingredients in bowl and mix. Let this sit together for a few hours for flavors to blend before serving. Store the salsa in an air-tight container in the fridge. It will keep for 1 to 2 weeks in the fridge.

SALADS AND DRESSINGS

Tabouli

So delicious, so nutritious! This is a great way to get those super-greens. Parsley and cilantro are both abundant in nutrients as well as great detoxifying herbs. Cilantro is particularly good at removing toxic heavy metals from the body.

1 bunch **Cilantro** - chopped
1 bunch **Parsley** - chopped
1 bunch **Green Onions** - sliced
2 **Tomatoes** - chopped
1 **Avocado** - chopped
½ c **Hemp Seeds** or Almonds – coarsely ground
2 T **Olive Oil**
½ **Lemon** - juiced
1 T **Agave** or Honey
1 t **Salt**
dash **Cayenne** – to taste

Mix lemon, olive oil, honey, salt and cayenne together in a bowl. Put the rest of salad ingredients in another bowl and pour dressing on top. Mix well and serve.

Beet Salad

I love beets and this is my favorite way to eat them! This salad is sweet as well as savory, and it is also really good spicy with extra cayenne added.

5 **Beets**, peeled
4 **Celery** stalks, finely chopped
2 **Apples**, peeled and cored
3 **Green Onions**, finely chopped
3 T **Parsley**, finely chopped
3 T **Olive Oil**
2 T **Apple Cider Vinegar**
½ t **Salt**
Dash **Cayenne**

Grate or process beets in food processor with S-blade until small chunks. Transfer to bowl. Likewise, grate or process apples. Add to bowl. Add the rest of ingredients and mix well. Let this sit for 1 hour before serving. Keeps well refrigerated for up to a week.

Cucumber Salad

This easy to make salad is attractive, delicious and especially good in the summer.

1 **English Cucumber** – quartered and sliced thin
¼ small **Red Onion** - chopped
¼ **Red Pepper** - chopped
leaves of 2 sprigs of **Cilantro**
2 T **Apple Cider Vinegar**
1 T **Agave**
½ t **Salt**
Dash **Cumin** and **Cayenne**

Mix all together in bowl. Let marinate at least an hour before serving.

Broccoli Salad

This beautiful colorful salad was one I ate a lot of when I first went raw. This salad keeps well for days in the refrigerator and so I would make large batches of it. It is still one that I make often. It is really nice with pieces chopped very small. The broccoli is easy to cut by holding the stem and chopping down from the tip of the head in small slices.

1 bunch **Broccoli** – chopped small
1 **Carrot** - grated
½ **Red Pepper** – chopped small
2 **Celery** Stalks – chopped small
3 **Green Onions** – chopped
½ c **Parsley** – chopped

Dressing:
1/3 c **Olive Oil**
¼ c **Water**
2 T **Balsamic Vinegar**
½ t **Dijon Mustard**
2 **Garlic** cloves- chopped
½ t **Natural Herbal Seasoning** blend, or add 1 t of mixed fresh Italian
herbs
½ t **Salt**
dash **Cayenne**

Put all salad ingredients in bowl. Pour dressing on top and mix together
well.

Daikon Radish Salad

This makes a great appetizer salad. Daikon radishes are a great cleanser
for the body!

1 small **Daikon Radish**, approximately 1 ½ c - grated
3 T **Apple Cider Vinegar**
2 T **Honey**, or Agave
Salt and **Cayenne** to taste

Mix all ingredients together in a bowl. Let marinate for an hour before
serving.

Singapore Seaweed Salad

This is the ultimate way to eat lots of sea vegetables. It is so delicious! And it is even better the following day so make lots.

½ c **Arame** or Hijiki - soak to rehydrate in a bowl of cool water for 15 to 30 minutes. Then rinse, drain and pat with a clean towel, or leave it sitting out in drainer for longer, to dry.
1 small **Cucumber** – peel, quarter lengthwise and remove seeds. Then cut into thin slices or matchsticks and pat dry.
½ c **Bean sprouts** – rinsed, drained and dried
½ **Red Pepper** – chopped
2 **Green Onions** – sliced

Dressing:
1 ½ T **Flax Oil**
1 ½ T **Sesame Oil**
2 T **Rice Vinegar,** or 1½ T Apple Cider Vinegar to keep the dish all-raw
1 T **Nama Shoyu**
1" **Ginger** – minced

Make dressing early so it has time to sit and for flavors to blend. Prepare the vegetables, keeping them as dry as possible, so that they dilute the dressing as little as possible. Toss salad ingredients all together with dressing. Top with Sesame seeds, if desired.

Autumn Harvest Vegetable Walnut Salad

This is a very hearty salad with a delicious creamy dressing. It is a warming and filling salad for the cooler fall weather.

1 **Carrot** – chopped
1 **Corn on the cob** - kernels cut off
4 **Mushrooms** – chopped
1 **Celery** stalk – chopped
½ c **Green Beans** – sliced
½ c **Walnuts** – crushed
1 **Green Onion** – sliced

Dressing:
2 T **Almond Butter**
1 T **Hemp Oil**
½ **Lemon** – juiced
1 ½ t **Nama Shoyu**
1 small **Garlic** clove – chopped
dash of **Chili powder**

Place all vegetables and walnuts in a bowl. Mix together dressing and pour over salad. Stir and Mix well and serve. This salad keeps well for a few days in the fridge.

Thai Marinated Broccoli

This is a great salad to take to friends, to parties and pot lucks. It is easy to make and it is usually a favorite. It also will last for several days in the fridge and is a great make-ahead salad.

1 head **Broccoli** - chopped
2 **Green Onions** - sliced
½ bunch **Cilantro** - chopped

Dressing:
1 T **Almond Butter**
1 T **Honey**
½ **Lemon** - juiced
1" **Ginger**, minced
1 to 2 cloves **Garlic**, minced
1 T **Nama Shoyu**
dash **Sambal Oelek,** or finely chopped Chili Peppers or Cayenne

Blend together dressing ingredients and then pour over vegetables. Stir to Mix well and let marinate for a few hours before serving. Will keep for several days refrigerated.

Colorful Veggie and Wild Rice Salad

This salad is so beautiful, like the colors of autumn. To me, it conjures up wild expressionistic paintings. It is sweet, crunchy, savory and very exciting.

1 c **Wild Rice** - soaked (sprouted) for 24 hrs
2 **Carrots** - chopped
2 **Celery** stalks - chopped
½ **Red Pepper** - chopped
2 **Green Onions** - sliced
¼ c **Raisins**

Dressing:
½ c **Olive Oil**
1 **Lemon** – juiced
1 T **Apple Cider Vinegar**
1 T **Maple Syrup** or raw Honey
½ t **Dijon Mustard,** or 1 t Mustard powder
1 **Garlic** clove
1 t **Salt**
Cayenne to taste

Blend dressing ingredients together and then mix in well with the rice and vegetables.

Gado Gado - Indonesian Salad

Gado Gado is a traditional Indonesian vegetable salad which is characterized by the *Peanut Sauce Dressing,* aka *Sambal Kecang,* which is served over it. Other vegetables such as: broccoli, celery, red pepper, green onion or watercress can be used in addition to, or instead of, the vegetables listed in the recipe.

4 c **Lettuce** – chopped
½ c **Carrots**- grated or slivered
½ c **Cabbage** – sliced or grated
½ c **Green Beans** or Long Beans – slivered
½ c **Tomato** – chopped
½ c **Bean Sprouts**
2" **Cucumber** –chopped
¼ c **Red Onion** – chopped

Place all salad ingredients together in a bowl. Serve with the following dressing.

Sambal Kecang - Peanut Sauce Dressing

This famous peanut sauce dressing is a favorite and ubiquitous sauce in Indonesia and Malaysia. It is traditionally served on *Gado Gado* and other mixed vegetable dishes, as well as just about everything. This raw version of the original has no peanuts in it but still has that peanut and distinctly Indonesian taste. This is a wonderful sauce served on spiralized vegetable noodles.

½ c **Almond Butter**
¼ c **Agave**
1 **Lemon** or Lime - juiced
2 T **Nama Shoyu**
1 T **Olive Oil**
½ T **Sesame Oil**
½ " **Ginger** – grated or minced
1 **Garlic** clove – minced
½ t **Sambal Oelek**, or ground Chilies or Chili powder
Salt and **Cayenne** to taste

Blend all ingredients together in bowl or a blender. This dressing is best served warm and can be warmed in a bowl which fits over a pot of boiling water. Stir so the bottom doesn't get too hot and the dressing is warm to the touch. Test with your finger, if it's too hot to touch it's destroying vital nutrients and enzymes.

Zesty Lemon House Dressing

This is a basic oil and lemon dressing which is an everyday favorite. This dressing is delicious on almost any salad.

½ c **Olive Oil**
1 **Lemon** – juiced
1 T **Apple Cider Vinegar**
3 T **Agave**
1 t **Salt**
1 t **Natural Herbal Seasoning** blend
½ t **Pepper**
2 T **Water**

Whisk all ingredients together in a bowl or blend in a blender. This dressing will keep for a month in a glass jar in the refrigerator.

Balsamic Vinaigrette

This classic dressing is not completely raw but you can make raw substitutions to it: agave for the maple syrup, mustard powder instead of the Dijon and apple cider vinegar or lemon juice instead of balsamic vinegar and although it will taste different it will still be delicious.

½ c **Olive Oil**
¼ c **Water**
2 T **Balsamic Vinegar**
2 T **Maple Syrup**
¼ t **Dijon Mustard**
1 **Garlic** clove
¾ t **Salt**
½ t **Natural Herbal Seasoning** blend
¼ t **Pepper**

Blend all ingredients together well. This vinaigrette will keep for a month in a glass jar in the refrigerator.

Olive Currant Nut and Seed Salad

This wonderful Italian salad has a sweet and salty richly flavoured combination of tastes from the currants, olives and pine nuts. It is complimented well with the *Balsamic Dressing* and also goes well with the *Zesty Lemon Dressing.*

4 c **Mixed Greens**
8 to 12 **Kalamata Olives** – pitted and halved
3 T **Currants**
3 T **Pine nuts**
3 T **Pumpkin seeds**
3 T **Hemp seeds**

Place all ingredients in a bowl and serve with your favorite dressing.

Strawberry Pecan Salad

This is so simple and easy, yet so beautiful and romantic and always one of my favorites!

1 big bowlful of **Baby Spinach** leaves
10 **Strawberries** – sliced
½ c **Pecans**
Optional – a handful of **Pumpkin Seeds**

Place in bowl and top with *Poppy seed Dressing*.

Poppy seed Dressing

This is a completely raw and absolutely delicious version. It is great on all salads but especially good on fruit based ones.

¼ c **Agave**
¼ c **Olive Oil**
¼ c **Water**
1 T **Apple Cider Vinegar**
2 T **Nama Shoyu**
2 T **Red Onion** - minced
2 T **Poppy seeds**
½ t **Mustard powder**
½ t **Paprika**

Whisk ingredients together in a bowl or blend all ingredients, except poppy seeds, together in a blender. After well blended, add poppy seeds and blend slowly to incorporate. This dressing will keep for several weeks to a month in the refrigerator.

Orange Salad

Simple, sweet and perfect when you are in a bright and happy orange mood!

½ bunch **Green Leaf Lettuce**
1 **Orange** – peeled, quartered and sliced
1 **Carrot** – peeled and grated
8 **Dates** – quartered lengthwise

Combine ingredients in bowl. Top with *Pear Dressing* and sprinkle some chopped nuts on top if desired.

Pear Dressing

This sweet dressing is also nice on many fruit salads as well as green salads with nuts and seeds.

1 **Pear**
½ **Orange** – juiced
¼ c **Olive Oil**
½ T **Honey**
Dash of **Salt**

Blend all ingredients together in a blender.
Store any leftovers in the fridge and use within a couple days.

Passion Berry Salad

Passion fruit has such a wonderful distinctive taste and goes so well with raspberries, and a great variety of fruit. Experiment with different types and combinations of fruit. It's fun to create new flavors and this is an easy recipe to work with.

4 **Pears** – chopped
2 c **Strawberries** – chopped
2 c **Grapes** – chopped

Dressing:
1 **Passion fruit**
½ c **Raspberries**
1 T **Agave**

Cut passion fruit in half and scoop out seeds with a spoon into a blender. Add raspberries and agave and blend all together. Pour dressing over cut up fruit. Stir to mix and serve.

CRACKERS AND PIZZA CRUST

Multi Seed Crackers

These crackers are not only delicious and flavorful but also incredibly healthy, filled with lots of super nutritious seeds and vegetables. They are vibrant and beautiful with their black sesame seeds and red tomato flecks.

1 c **Flax** - soaked in 2 c water a couple hours before mixing
½ c **Pumpkin seeds** – soaked
½ c **Sunflower seeds** – soaked
1/3 c **Black Sesame seeds**
1/3 c **Sun-dried Tomatoes**, approximately 12
3 **Green Onions** – chopped fine
½ **Celery** stalk – chopped fine
2 **Garlic** cloves – minced
1 t **Turmeric**
1 t **Salt**
½ t **Cumin**
½ t **Chili powder**
¼ t **Celery salt**
¼ t **Cayenne**

Blend all ingredients together in a food processor. Add water, if needed. Press mixture flat onto teflex sheets, quite thin, about 1/6" thick. Score the size of cracker you want with the edge of a dull knife or spatula. Dehydrate at 115 degrees overnight. Flip over unto a mesh screen and continue to dry another 6 to 8 hours, or until crisp. Store crackers in a container or zip lock bag in a cool dry place. They will keep well for weeks and keep freshest and longer if kept in an air tight container.

Honey Crackers

Simple and sweet! These crackers make a great snack all on their own.

2 c **Golden Flax seed** – soaked for a couple hours in 3 c Water
1 c **Golden Flax seed** – ground
½ c **Honey**
2 t **Cinnamon**
2 t **Salt**

Process all ingredients together in food processor. Add more water if necessary to make mixture wet enough to spread easily. Spread quite thinly onto teflex sheets and dehydrate for 3 to 4 hours. Flip onto mesh screen and continue dehydrating for 10 to 12 hours. These crackers will keep well for several weeks, stored covered in container or plastic bag and kept in a dry cool place.

Mexican Nut and Seed Crackers

Crackers can be a staple food in a raw lifestyle. These Mexican ones are delicious and a favorite. They are very flavorful, but not too spicy – unless you want them to be!

1 ½ c **Walnuts** – soaked
1 ½ c **Sunflower seeds** - soaked
1 ½ c **Pumpkin seeds** – soaked
2 c Yellow **Flax seeds** – ground
1 c Yellow **Flax seeds** – soaked in 2 c water
½ c **Sun-dried Tomatoes** – soaked 2-4 hours
1 **Red Pepper**
½ **Lime** – juiced
1 T **Agave**
1 **Jalapeno**
2 **Garlic** cloves
¼ c **Cilantro** chopped
2 t each **Salt**, **Chili powder**, **Cumin** and **Onion powder**
4 to 6 **Basil** leaves or 1 T dried
4 to 6 **Oregano** stems, remove stalks and use leaves, or 2 t dried
Dash **Cayenne**

Process all ingredients together in food processor. Add tomato soak water as necessary to make the mixture wet enough to spread easily. Spread quite thinly onto teflex sheets and dehydrate for 3 to 4 hours. Flip onto mesh screen and continue dehydrating for 10 to 12 hours. Let cool and then break into pieces and store in air tight container or zip lock bag. These will keep for several weeks to one month if well dried.

Herb and Onion Crackers

These crackers can be varied greatly depending on the herbs used. If you like dill try a batch using lots of dill and parsley, or try rosemary, tarragon and chives together or an Italian combination with lots of oregano and basil. The options are plentiful. Have fun and enjoy!

1 c **Pumpkin seeds**
1 c **Sunflower seeds**
2 c **Brown Flax seeds** – soaked in 3 c water for 2 to 4 hours
2 c **Brown Flax seeds** - ground
2 c **Zucchini** – cubed, or substitute with Cauliflower, Broccoli, Carrot or Squash – chopped
1 c **Mixed Herbs**, such as: Cilantro, Basil, Dill, Oregano, Rosemary, Marjoram, Chives or Parsley – chopped
1 c **Red Onion** - minced
½ **Lemon** – juiced
1 T **Nama Shoyu**
1 T **Agave**
1 **Garlic** clove- minced
2 t **Salt**
1 t **Cumin**
1 t **Chili powder**

Process seeds until coarsely chopped in a food processor; transfer to bowl. Process vegetables with the rest of ingredients until well chopped and then add to bowl with seeds. Stir to mix all ingredients well together. Spread mixture ¼" thick onto teflex sheets and dehydrate for 3 to 4 hours. Flip onto mesh screen and continue dehydrating for 10 to 12 hours. Let cool and then break into pieces and store in air tight container or zip lock bag. These will keep for several weeks to 1 month if well dried.

Veggie Seed Pizza Crust

This pizza crust is made about twice as thick as the cracker recipes and has lots of almonds and vegetables in it for a subtly delicious flavor and a softer texture.

1½ c **Almonds**, ground
3 **Carrots**, ground
1 **Zucchini** - chopped
¾ c **Flax seeds -** soaked in 1 c water for a few hours
½ c **Pumpkin seeds**
½ c **Sunflower seeds**
½ c **Olive Oil**
½ t **Salt**

Finely grind almonds and carrots in a food processor. Transfer to bowl. Grind zucchini and seeds in processor until coarse. Stop and scrape down sides and add flax seeds; process 10 seconds. Transfer to bowl. Mix oil and salt into mixture in bowl, combining well. Spread mixture out ¼" thick onto teflex sheets. Score into desired size. Dehydrate at 110 degrees overnight, approximately 8 hours. Then flip onto mesh screen, remove teflex and continue dehydrating for 3 to 4 hours or until dry. This pizza crust will keep for up to a month covered and kept in fridge.

Cookies, Bars and Dehydrated Snacks

A dehydrator is best for these recipes. See the resource section for more information on dehydrating. However, it is possible to dry these recipes in a warm oven with the door open just a bit. Set the oven to warm, not too hot, as the goal is to keep it below 115 degrees Fahrenheit. In hot climates it is also possible to sun-dry these treats outside.

Rawkalicious Cookies

These superfood cookies are a favorite and make an incredible breakfast or quick on-the-go snack. They taste delicious and they are full of nutrients. It's a win-win situation!

When making these cookies, mix, form and then dehydrate right away in order for them to stay a light color. The mashed banana in the recipe will turn dark if it sits in the air and oxidizes for a long period. This will not harm the flavor or the quality, only their appearance, the cookies will turn out darker.

1 c **Almond pulp** - from making almond milk, or grind dry almonds into flour
1 c **Walnuts** – crushed
2 **Bananas** – mashed
½ c **Currants**
½ c **Sesame seeds**
½ c **Coconut flakes**
½ c **Cacao nibs**
½ c **Pumpkin seeds**
¼ c **Goji Berries**
¼ c **Honey**
¼ c **Hemp seeds**
1 t **Vanilla**
½ t **Cinnamon**

Soak pumpkin seeds and goji berries together in a bowl with just enough water to cover them for a couple hours. Mix the rest of the ingredients in another mixing bowl. Drain and add the gojis & pumpkin seeds. Mix well. Drop by spoonfuls onto teflex and slightly flatten. Dehydrate for 4 to 6 hours at 115 degrees. Flip onto mesh screen and continue dehydrating for another 10 to 12 hours, until dry. Enjoy!

Coconut Almond Caramel Cookies

This cookie has a sweet lightly spiced irresistible caramel flavor, which is quite delicious. Just a little maple syrup is added for flavor, which is not raw and can be substituted for agave or honey if preferred.

3 c dried shredded **Coconut**
1 ½ c **Dates**
1 c **Almond flour** - finely ground almonds
¼ c **Almond Butter**
¼ c **Maple Syrup**
1 T **Coconut Oil**
1 T **Vanilla**
½ T **Cinnamon**
1 t **Nutmeg**
½ t **Salt**

Blend all ingredients together in food processor. Drop by spoonful's onto teflex sheets and lightly press to flatten. Dehydrate for 3 to 4 hours on teflex at 115 degrees, then flip onto mesh screen & continue drying overnight.

Fudge Cookies

I love raw chocolate fudge cookies. They are sweet, chewy, taste fantastic and on top of it all, they are bursting with nutrition!

1 ½ c **Walnuts** - soaked
1 ½ c **Cashews** – soaked
1 c **Dates**
½ c raw **Cacao powder** or ground Cacao nibs
¼ c **Maple Syrup** or Agave
1 T **Coconut Oil**
1 t **Vanilla**
½ t **Salt**

dash of **Cinnamon**

Rinse and drain nuts well and process with the rest of ingredients in a food processor. Remove by spoonfuls onto teflex sheet and dehydrate for 4 to 6 hours at 115 degrees. Flip onto mesh screen & continue drying a few more hours until the outside is dry but they are still moist.

Apple Oatmeal Cookies

If you mix these up and put them in the dehydrator in the evening so that thy will be ready in to eat in the morning you will be very happy you did! And your kitchen will smell amazing.

1 c **Oat Groats** – ground into flour
1 c **Walnuts**
1 c **Almonds**
½ c **Raisins**
4 **Apples** – peeled and cored
½ c **Maple Syrup** or Agave
1 T **Cinnamon**
1 t **Vanilla**
½ t **Salt**

Grind oat groats in a high speed blender or a coffee or spice grinder and transfer to bowl. Grind almonds in a blender or process in a food processor until finely ground and then add to ground oats in bowl. Process walnuts until coarsely ground in processor and add to bowl. Next place the raisins, apples and the rest of the ingredients in the processor and puree until raisins are coarsely chopped. Add to mixture in bowl and stir to combine well. Drop by spoonfuls onto a teflex sheet, press down slightly, until approx ½" to ¾" high. Dehydrate at 115 degrees for 4 to 6 hours and then flip onto mesh screen and continue dehydrating 8 to 12 hours until dry. Remove and store in container at room temperature for several days or in the fridge for up to 2 weeks.

'Red Moon Rising' Lemon Raspberry Cookies

These cookies are very flavorful and the lemon and raspberry flavors go together beautifully. They are delicious and can be garnished with a little sprinkle of shredded coconut on top.

Lemon cookie:
2 c **Cashews**
2 c **Coconut**
½ c **Lemon juice**
¼ c **Lemon zest**
¼ c **Agave**

Raspberry Topping:
1 c **Raspberries**

¼ c **Agave**
1 T **Lemon juice**
2 T **Psyllium**
a dash of **Salt**

Blend raspberry topping ingredients together in a blender and set aside. Add all of the ingredients for lemon cookies in a food processor and process all together until well combined. Form into balls, slightly flatten and press in an indent in the top. Fill indent with 1 tablespoon of raspberry topping. These can be eaten just like this or dehydrated for a few hours to make a drier cookie.

Decadent Vanilla Hemp Bars

I love having a bar recipe made ahead and always having them available. I usually have a container of bars kept in the fridge. Thy are great to have as a snack, for breakfast or to take when you are on the go and have with you, so you are always prepared for when you get hungry.

2 c **Cashews** - ground into flour
1 c **Hemp seeds**
1 c **Honey Dates**
¼ c **Coconut Oil**
1 T **Vanilla**

Blend altogether in food processor. Press out flat onto teflex sheet ½" high. Press extra hemp seeds into the top if desired. Score into bar size with a knife. Dehydrate for 2 hours at 115 degrees. Flip and dehydrate another 2 to 4 hours. Let cool, Break apart and Enjoy!

Fruit, Seed and Nut Bars

This recipe makes lots as I tend to make a big batch less frequently. These are great to have on hand. They keep well and make a great on-the-go snack.

1½ c **Almonds**
½ c **Hazelnuts** or Pecans or Cashews
2 c **Sesame seeds**
½ c **Pumpkin seeds**
½ c **Sunflower seeds**
1 c **Dates**
1 ½ c **Raisins**
1 ½ c other **Dried Fruit** of choice, such as: Apricots,
Blueberries, Cherries, Cranberries
1 c **Honey**
1 t **Salt**

Pulse chop almonds and hazelnuts in processor until small pieces and then put in bowl. Pulse-chop the sunflower and pumpkin seeds and add them to bowl. Chop dates and any larger dried fruit and add these to bowl. Add the rest of the ingredients and mix well. Spread out onto teflex sheets ½ to ¾" thick and score into bars. Dehydrate at 110 degrees overnight, approximately 8 hours. Then flip onto mesh screen, remove teflex and continue dehydrating for 3 to 4 hours or until dry. These keep well stored in an air-tight container in a cold, dry place or in the fridge. They will keep well for at least a month properly stored.

Kale Chips

This snack can easily take the place of potato chips. They are flavorful, salty and have a great crunch. They are delicious and so easy to make. What a great way to eat a lot of kale at one sitting!

1 bunch **Kale**
2 T **Olive Oil**
1 t **Salt**
½ t **Onion powder**
½ t **Garlic powder**
½ t **Chili powder**
½ t **Cumin**
½ t **Cayenne**

Mix olive oil with spices together in a large bowl and set aside. Prepare kale by cutting hard middle stalk from kale and cutting leaves into a few large pieces. I usually cut the large leaves into 4 to 6 pieces. Add kale to bowl and use hands to mix and massage oil and spices into the kale leaves to cover completely. Place kale leaves onto mesh sheets and dehydrate at 115 degrees overnight, or for 6 to 8 hours.

Desserts

The dessert section is where raw foods really come out on top. People are always so amazed when they discover how incredibly delicious raw desserts can be. Taste great, look amazing! Yes, you can have your raw cake and eat it too!

Apple Pie

This apple pie is as delicious as any baked apple pie I have ever had. I find it quite incredible and wonderful to have nutritious healthy desserts that can rival our traditional and generally quite unhealthy cooked ones. The raisins get processed and are almost indistinguishable in the final product, but they are what give most of the sweetness to the pie. The psyllium husk gives the filing its firmness after it sets so it is easy and beautiful to cut and present.

4 **Apples** - peeled, slice 3 cups of apple and set aside
½ c **Raisins**
½ c **Agave**
½ **Lemon** - juiced
3 T **Psyllium husk**
½ T **Cinnamon**
¼ t **Nutmeg**
Dash of **Allspice** and **Salt**

Have the pie crust made and ready first. Process all ingredients together, except for the 3 cups of sliced apples set aside, in a food processor. Transfer mixture to bowl and add the reserved sliced apples and mix well to combine. Pour this pie filling into a crust, spread to the edges and flatten down the top and allow to set for an hour before serving. Makes one pie. This can be frozen and thawed to serve at a later time.

Coconut Seed Crust

This crust is delicious and goes so well with the apple pie filling. How wonderful to have a pie crust that is so good for you!

1 ¼ c **Coconut**
1 c **Sunflower seeds**
½ c **Dates**
2 T **Honey**
½ t **Vanilla**
Dashes of **Cinnamon** and **Salt**

Coarsely chop the sunflower seeds in a food processor. Add the rest of the ingredients to the processor and combine well. Lightly oil a pie pan with coconut oil and then transfer the filling into it, pressing down to form crust. Because of the sensitive nature of flax seeds, a pie made with this crust should be stored in the refrigerator and eaten within 3 to 4 days.

Date Squares

This is a classic and it turns out that the new raw version is just as great as the original version. These remind me of my childhood and having tea with my grandma. They were always a family favorite and bring back great memories.

Crust:
1 c **Almonds**
1 c **Pecans** or Walnuts or a combination of both
1 c **Oat flour** - ground oat groats
¼ c **Maple Syrup** or Agave
1 t **Cinnamon**
1 t **Vanilla**

Filling:
1½ c **Honey Dates**
1 to 2 **Apples** - peeled and cored

Line an 8"x 8" square pan with wax or parchment paper.

Process the nuts in a food processor until coarsely ground. Make oat flour by grinding oat groats in a blender or coffee grinder. Put all of the crust ingredients in a bowl and mix together well. Press half of this mixture into the lined pan.

Puree the apple and dates together in a food processor. Spread apple date mixture over the bottom crust and then top with the remaining crust mixture. Loosen with knife around any edges where there is no parchment paper lining it. Place a cutting board over the top of the pan and holding both together flip over. Remove pan and paper and cut into squares. The squares can be eaten as is or set them into the dehydrator and dehydrated for 1 to 3 hours to dry slightly. If the cutting board is small enough I often just set the whole cutting board in with the date squares still on it.

Raspberry Coconut Squares

This is a scrumptious layered dessert which is perfect on its own or you could take it further and top each serving with a spoonful of *Macadamia or Cashew Cream.*

Base:
¾ c **Oat flour** - ground oat groats
½ c **Walnuts** - soaked
½ c **Almonds** – soaked
2 T **Maple Syrup**
½ t **Vanilla**
½ t **Cinnamon**

Middle:
1 c **Raspberries**
1 c **Macadamias** or **Cashews** – soaked 2 hours to soften
1 **Banana**
¼ c **Agave**
1 T **Psyllium**

Top:
1 c **Coconut** – dried, shredded
1 c **Walnuts**
¼ c **Honey Dates,** approximately 8
2 T **Maple Syrup**
½ **Lemon** – juiced
2 t **Lemon** zest
½ t **Vanilla**
dash of **Salt**

Process the base ingredients together in a food processor just until it starts sticking together and forming a ball. Press into a square 8"x 8" pan which has been lightly oiled with coconut oil. Set aside. Blend the ingredients for the middle raspberry filling layer together in a blender. After they are well pureed, spread on top of the base layer in the pan. Set the pan in the freezer to set for an hour. Process the topping ingredients together in a food processor. Spoon this mixture on top of the middle layer, spreading it out flat. Sprinkle with coconut and press into top. Return to pan to the fridge or freezer to set for a half hour and then take out, cut into squares and serve. These will keep well in the fridge covered for over a week.

Mango Tarts

A sweet tropical sunshine dessert that is so delicious you will want to have a party and share these with all your friends. Everyone will love them, so you may want to double the recipe!

Shell crust:
½ c **Macadamia nuts**
2 c shredded **Coconut**
½ c **Honey**
½ **Lemon**, juiced

Filling:
1 c **Mango**
½ c **Pineapple**
8 **Dates**

Process the shell crust ingredients in a food processor until fine. Press into tart pans or a small muffin tin, making a hollow part in the middle for the filling. Blend together the filling ingredients in a blender or processor. Spoon filling into the hollowed out area of tart shells and then let set for an hour. Carefully remove from tin and serve.

Tropical Fruit Cobbler

Enjoy a tantalizing taste of the tropics with this great twist on the classic favorite.

Fruit Base:
1 **Banana** – peeled & broken into large pieces
1 **Mango** peeled, pitted and diced
1 c **Pineapple** chunks
1 c **Papaya** chunks
½ **Lime** – juiced
2 t **Psyllium**

Topping:
1 c **Macadamia**
½ c **Walnuts**
½ c **Almonds** – soaked
½ c dried shredded **Coconut**
1 c **Dates**
1 t **Vanilla**

Process fruit just until the pieces are still in fairly large to medium size (¼" to ½") chunks. Mix psyllium and lime juice into fruit and pour into the bottom of an 8" x 8" pan and pat down flat.

Process the nuts and dates in a food processor until still coarse and chunky. Add the rest of the ingredients and pulse chop in together until still just coarsely chopped and mixed in thoroughly. Sprinkle the nut and date topping layer over the fruit base evenly and press down gently to cover and flatten. Sprinkle some coconut flakes on top. Serve and Enjoy!

Macadamia or Cashew Cream

This is a great topping or icing and can be used on many desserts, or just eaten with a spoon!

Create a beautiful parfait by alternating layers of this cream and fresh cut up berries or fruit. Layer them on a 45 degree angle for added presentation. Finish off with this cream and one fruit slice or berry on top.

½ c **Macadamias** or **Cashews** – soaked 2 or more hours and drained
2 **Medjool Dates**
½ **Lemon** – juiced
1 t **Vanilla**
Water, approximately 3 T

Blend all ingredients except water in the blender. Add water slowly until desired consistency is reached, being careful not to add too much water. Stop and check periodically. If the cream is too stiff, continue blending and slowly adding more water. Cream should be fluffy and smooth when done. It is best used right away.

Brownies

One of the best desserts ever created and the raw version is so simple to make. Chocolate Heaven!

2 c **Walnuts**
2 c **Dates**
1 c **Cacao powder**
1 t **Vanilla**
½ t **Cinnamon**

Process all ingredients together in a food processor. Stop when it is well broken down but still crumbly. Test to see if it holds together by pinching a bit of the mixture in your fingers. These brownies are very easy to make but the key is to stop processing at just the right time. You want to stop the processor before the mixture forms together in a ball when it is processing. It will still look loose and crumbly at the perfect stage. At this point, transfer to and spread it out in a pan, which has been lightly oiled with coconut oil. Top with *Creamy Chocolate Icing*, if desired. Cut into squares, remove from pan and serve.

Variation: **Coconut Brownies** - Add 1 c Coconut and ¼ c Dates to the *Brownies* recipe and follow directions as stated.

Creamy Chocolate Icing

This easy to make icing is deliciously decadent!

Sometimes I make a small bowl of this in the morning and stir in lots of superfoods, powered herbs and medicinal mushrooms and eat it with a spoon. Even with all these things poured in, it still tastes just like creamy rich chocolate icing. Now that's a great way to start the day!

½ c **Cacao powder**
¼ c **Honey** or **Agave**
¼ c **Almond Butter**
¼ t **Vanilla**

Mix honey, almond butter and vanilla together in a bowl. Slowly mix in the chocolate powder until it forms a creamy smooth icing.

Cinnamon Chocolate Balls

Sweet, delicious and nutritious! An easy to make power snack which doubles as a great dessert.

2 c **Almonds**
1 c **Dates**
½ c **Cacao**
¼ c **Goji Berries**
1 t **Vanilla**
1 t **Cinnamon,** and more for rolling in
Water – if necessary

Process all ingredients together in food processor. Add water if you need more moisture to process and until you have dough that is pliable. Form dough into balls and roll in cinnamon.

ICE CREAM

These are some of the most basic, as well as my favorite, ice cream flavors. They are the ultimate in delicious ice cream recipes and are all non-dairy and vegan. Raw ice cream is as creamy, dreamy and supremely delicious as any. In fact I find raw ice cream superior with its fresh clean and rich flavors coming through.

Almonds can be substituted for cashews in all of the ice cream recipes, but it is best to soak and blanch the almonds first to remove the skins, especially for the vanilla and strawberry flavors.

Vanilla Coconut Ice Cream

Warning: This ice cream is so creamy and so deliciously decadent that it is hard to stop eating!

2 c **Cashews** – soaked
1 c **Young Thai Coconut** meat, see note below if not available
2 c **Water**, use Coconut water if available
1 ½ c **Agave**
½ c **Maple Syrup**
1 T **Vanilla**

Note: Maple syrup is not raw. To keep this completely raw, substitute agave. Unpasteurized honey can be substituted also but will give a 'honey' flavor.

Blend drained cashews and coconut meat with water in a high speed blender. Add the vanilla and agave and continue blending until it reaches a smooth and creamy consistency. Transfer mixture to an electric ice cream maker and process according to manufacturer's instructions. When finished, transfer to air tight containers (glass being preferable to plastic) and then set containers into the freezer.

Option - If young Thai Coconuts are not available, substitute with one additional cup of Cashews and a half cup of Coconut Oil.

Option - Cashews can be substituted with Almonds which have been soaked at least 4 hours and blanched.

Option – Maple syrup can be substituted for Date paste made by blending 2/3 cup dates with 1 cup of water. It can also be substituted with more Agave.

Maple Pecan Ice Cream

Substitute the Agave for **Maple Syrup** and add 1 cup of **Pecans**.

Chocolate Cookie Explosion Ice Cream

This decadent chocolate creation is my favorite flavor. It's hard to go wrong with all that chocolate! The best thing is that it is made with raw cacao which is abundantly nutritious and so this is virtually guilt free. This is a really fun recipe to experiment and try different variations with, but this combination is my winner.

3 c **Cashews** - soaked
2 c **Water**
½ c **Coconut Oil**
1 c **Maple Syrup**
1 c **Agave**
1 t **Vanilla**
½ c **Cacao powder**
½ c **Cacao nibs**
½ c *Brownies* or *Fudge Cookie* pieces – chopped

note: Maple syrup is not raw. To keep this completely raw, substitute with agave. Unpasteurized honey can be substituted also but will give a 'honey' flavor.

Blend cashews with water in a high speed blender until smooth and creamy. Add the coconut oil, maple syrup, agave, vanilla and chocolate powder and continue blending until well mixed. Into this mixture add cacao nibs and brownie or cookie pieces. Transfer this mixture into an electric ice cream maker and process according to manufacturer's instructions. When finished, transfer to air tight containers and set into the freezer.

Black Forest Ice Cream

Add ½ cup of **Cherries** in addition to or instead of the Brownie or Cookie pieces.

Chocolate Caramel Fudge Ice Cream

Add ½ c **Maca**. This will give the ice cream a caramel flavor.

Strawberry Ice Cream

This raw strawberry ice cream recipe is a classic favorite and extra delicious made with fresh strawberries. This is heavenly made with strawberries in season and at their most flavorful.

2 c **Cashews**
2 c **Strawberries**
1 c **Agave**
1 c **Water**
¼ c **Coconut Butter**
2 T **Vanilla**

Blend all ingredients in a blender until smooth. Chill in the refrigerator and then transfer to an electric ice cream maker and process according to manufacturer's instructions. When finished, transfer into containers and freeze until firm and ready to eat. Enjoy!

7 INGREDIENTS

This list includes some of the more interesting and lesser common foods used in these recipes. It also includes non-raw foods which are sometimes used in small quantities in certain recipes for flavor, binding or to enhance the recipe in some way. Usually in a recipe containing these, it is indicated as not raw and an alternative whenever possible is given.

Agave - is a natural alternative to sugar which is healthy and has a very low glycemic index. It comes from the same plant that tequila is derived from, a member of the lily and amaryllis family, found in the southern US, Mexico and South America. It is very sweet and has a mild taste which is beneficial for many recipes. The darker agave usually has a stronger taste. Make sure the label states that it is raw, some are not. Agave can be found in most health food stores.

Almond Butter - Raw almond butter is very flavorful: delicious and sweet. It is convenient to have on hand as a quick spread or for use in recipes. To make almond milk quickly; blend 1 tablespoon of almond butter with 1 cup of water. When buying almond butter make sure that it is raw and not roasted, organic and made with only almonds and without preservatives, additives, chemicals or sugar. This can be found in some supermarkets, most health food stores or ordered online. For listings of my favorite brands check Resources.

Bee Pollen – is one of nature's most complete, nutritionally dense foods which contain almost every nutrient we need to survive.

Cacao – raw cacao beans are 100% pure, straight from nature, bittersweet chocolate. Cacao is filled with a multitude of health boosting and feel-good properties and has been treasured and revered for centuries. Most of the processed chocolate on the market is but a vague memory of the real thing. In the last few years cacao has been becoming more and more popular with its healing benefits being studied and recognized. For most recipes in this book calling for cacao a raw cacao mass, which is fresh beans ground and allowed to re-harden, is used. To use this I usually let sit in a bowl over hot water until it is a soft, liquid paste form. If raw cacao mass is not available, Raw cacao or chocolate powder can be used.

Cacao Butter – This is the oil which is separated from the cacao bean. It usually comes in a hard, light beige-ivory colored, block. This ingredient is usually used in desserts and will make them more rich and creamy. To use in recipes, bring to a liquid form first by heating slowly. I usually do this in a bowl sitting over a pan of hot water but it can also be done by placing in a warm place for a longer period of time. You will have to keep warm or work quickly with it as it hardens again quickly.

Cayenne – The dried and ground red cayenne chili pepper is used by raw foodists in much the same way black pepper is used, with salt, as a condiment, sprinkled on top of foods for extra flavor. While black pepper is carcinogenic, not healthy, cayenne has been used medicinally for centuries and has many health benefits. It is beneficial for the whole digestive system and also the heart and the circulatory system. It acts as a catalyst and increases the effectiveness of other foods eaten with it.

Coconuts – Generally come in 3 ways. The mature small brown coconut, which is most common and easiest to find, is available in most supermarkets, the young Thai coconut, which has its white pulp often cut around it and is wrapped in plastic. This type has soft coconut meat inside which is soft and can be eaten with a spoon. This type is best for most recipes but can be harder to find. They are usually found in Asian grocery stores and occasionally in supermarkets and health food stores. Thirdly there is the green coconut, this comes to you straight as it falls from the tree and although it is usually the hardest to find it is often freshest. The meat inside this whole coconut can be either thin which you can spoon out to very thin and gelatinous to non-existent, but it will be filled with lots of coconut water. Coconut water along with mother's breast milk are two of the very few substances known to contain lauric acid which is a powerful immunity booster. It is also one of the highest sources of electrolytes known to man. The coconut meat is mainly made up of healthy medium chain fatty acids which are good for you and will most likely get used for energy instead of getting stored in the body. It even helps to release stored fats – Bonus! Young coconuts are the most health enhancing. Coconut meat freezes well.

Coconut Oil – stays in harder, in a butter form, when cool but its melting point is 70 to 75 degrees F and when it gets warm and above this temperature it will turn into an oil. Coconut oil contains a naturally saturated fat, made up of healthy medium chain fatty acids, which are very good for you.

Coconut Cream - This can be made by blending mature coconut meat with coconut oil or can be bought pre-made and bottled.

Coconut Milk – is made by blending the pulp of mature coconuts with water and straining.

Coconut Water – is the liquid found naturally inside the coconut.

Dried Fruits – The brightly colored dried fruits are often heavily treated with sulphites, preservatives and refined sugars. Stick to the organic and darker ones, which although not as nice looking, are much more flavorful and better for your health.

Dates - Stock up on dates, which can be eaten as they come and which are used in many desserts and recipes as a sweetener. Dates have the highest concentration of fruit sugars of any fruit. There are over 400 varieties of dates, but only a few types are found here. Honey dates are smaller, cheaper and more commonly found. Medjool dates are big and plump when fresh. They are more expensive and have a fantastic taste. When not indicated, recipes ask for honey dates, but Medjool can always be substituted and slightly less may be required. Make sure dates are pitted before using.

Garlic – is one of the most powerful plant medicines. For great health eat this as often as possible.

Ginger – is a warming and cleansing herb which stimulates blood flow and increases the absorption of nutrients from foods eaten with it. Ginger freezes well; peel and store in the freezer, when it is needed, remove, grate amount required and return to freezer.

Herbs – are always best fresh when possible. However, if not indicated, recipes will assume that dried is being used. If using fresh, use twice the indicated measurement. Likewise if a recipe asks for fresh and it is unavailable use half the amount of the dried herb. I usually always have fresh cilantro, basil and parsley on hand, often mint and in season a multitude, which can be picked and used fresh from the garden: oregano, chives, rosemary, thyme, dill. Use organic herbs whenever possible as conventional herbs are often sprayed heavily with a wide assortment of pesticides, herbicides, fungicides, insecticides and other harmful chemicals. Also, afterwards they are often sterilized or irradiated with the gas ethylene oxide, which is highly toxic. If you do use conventionally grown herbs, make sure they are washed well before using.

Honey – Make sure to buy unpasteurized honey, which is raw and commonly found in health food stores. Try to find a local source of it which is produced in a clean environment away from the city. Honey has been used since ancient times both as a food and as a medicine. It has many health benefits; it is loaded with enzymes and contains several strains of friendly bacteria, both lactobacilli and bifidobacteria. It has antibacterial properties and contains antioxidants and flavonoids. Honey comes in a range of colors and flavors depending on the type of flowers from which it was made, such as: alfalfa, heather, acacia, manuka, thyme and lavender.

Lecithin – A supplement made from soybeans. It is useful to make recipes smooth and creamy and also used to bind oil and water together. Find an organic, non GMO, source.

Maca – A Peruvian root which is sold dried and powdered. Gives stamina and energy and has feel-good and aphrodisiacal properties. It is also reputed to build muscle and balance hormones. This is a real superfood which I try to include in my diet each day. You can add it to smoothies and desserts. It has a caramel-like flavor which goes well with chocolate, but it is usually included as a nutritional boost rather than for its flavor.

Maple Syrup – This is the boiled sap of Maple trees which is collected in the spring. Although it is not raw, it does contain some minerals and more nutrients than most processed sweeteners, and it is a delicious and distinct flavor which is sometimes used as a condiment and flavoring with raw dishes. If you prefer to stay completely raw, other raw sweeteners such as agave, honey or dates can be substituted in recipes.

Miso – A fermented food made from rice, barley or, most commonly, soybeans, and sea salt, which has been a part of Japanese cuisine and culture for centuries. While not raw, the fermenting process makes it living and gives it an abundance of beneficial microorganisms, it also is loaded with vitamins, minerals, essential oils and the highest quality protein; it contains all of the essential amino acids. There is an extremely wide variety of miso available. Miso comes in different varieties and flavors which range from salty, sweet, earthy, fruity, and savory and different colors from dark to red to white mellow miso. Most recipes in this book are made with a white mellow miso.

Mushrooms – There are thousands of types of edible mushrooms which are regularly harvested. There are many medicinal mushrooms which are a great benefit to assist and strengthen the body but which are not commonly used in creating raw dishes, such as Reishi, Cordycepts and Maitake, amongst many others.

Listed here are a few of the most used and interesting of the culinary mushrooms:

Chanterelle - Have a distinctive vase-shape with curled edges. Although they come in a variety of colors, the white, yellow and orange are more common. They have a delicate texture and a nutty, almost peppery flavor.

Crimini – Its appearance is similar to the common white mushroom except that it is brown. Its flavor is slightly more intense and earthy.

Enoki - are very small, whitish-yellowish, and grow in tight clusters of long leggy stems growing together topped with tiny white caps. They are very tender when raw but they get tough when cooked. They have a mild, subtle flavor which is very delicious. They can be used in many dishes: add to miso soup before serving, on top of salads, in sandwiches, as pizza toppings and for garnishing.

Morels – are an unusual looking mushroom with a brown, distinctively honeycomb texture, cone shaped cap and short stem. These are the most easily identifiable of wild mushrooms and often found commercially as dried. When found and used fresh, like Truffles, they are considered a rare and prized delicacy.

Oyster – These mushrooms are commonly used in Chinese and Japanese cuisine. They have a distinctive flavor similar to Chanterelles. They are the most diversely colored and are commonly found as white, yellow, pink, grey, brown, and black.

Portobello – Are mature versions of the crimini mushroom and the largest of edible mushrooms, This flavorful mushroom is characterized by its very large brown cap which can be up to six inches in diameter. They have a hearty flavor and they marinate well. Also because of their size they are great for stuffing.

Shitake – In addition to their distinctive delicious flavor, shitakes have many medicinal, especially immunological, benefits. The stems are harder than the soft fleshy caps and are often not used for culinary purposes.

Truffles – Cannot be easily harvested and are very expensive. Black truffles are far less pungent and more refined than white truffles.

White (Agaricus) – The most common mushroom available in many sizes from a small 'button' size to very large. They have a very mild flavor.

Nama Shoyu – Nama means raw in Japanese. This is the only raw, unpasteurized soy sauce available. It is made from organic soybeans, wheat, mountain spring water and salt in the traditional way; it is naturally aged for four years in cedar kegs. This is the most delicious soy sauce and is the most loaded with enzymes and lactobacillus and other beneficial organisms.

Nutritional Yeast – Although this yeast has nutritional benefits, it is very rich in vitamins, including B12, and amino acids; it is usually used in recipes for its slightly cheesy flavor. It is sold both as yellowish flakes or powder and is available at most health food stores, usually in bulk. It has a long shelf life and will stay good for over a year.

Nuts and Seeds – These include: Almonds, Brazil nuts, Cashews, Walnuts, Pecans, Pine nuts, Pistachios, Hazelnuts and Pumpkin seeds, Sunflower seeds, Sesame seeds, Chia seeds, Flax seeds, Hemp seeds and more. Have a large selection of nuts in stock, especially when first going raw. While not a good idea to eat large quantities of these, in the beginning most people when going raw will eat more. Recipes with these will help fill you up and give you that 'full' feeling most people are used to when eating a lot of cooked foods. Nuts and seeds can be stored in bags in the refrigerator, unless they will be used soon after purchasing. They can go rancid, especially nuts and seeds with a high oil content, when they are contact with a lot of light and heat. Large quantities can be stored in the freezer. Seeds can be stored in cupboards, but it is best to keep them away from light as much as possible.

Oat Groats – this is how oats come in their raw form. They are often steamed, but can be purchased raw. Oat groats can be soaked and sprouted for 24 to 48 hours prior to using for increased nutrition. Steel cut oats are oat groats that have been cut into a smaller pieces and are generally kept and sold still in their raw state. Rolled oats are more commonly found in grocery stores and are always steamed and not raw. Oat groats can be found in some supermarkets but are more readily found in many health food stores.

Oils – are extracted from their natural sources, from fruits, vegetables, nuts and seeds.

Olive oil is the most commonly used and diversified oil. It is a staple and can be used in almost any recipe. Store in a cool dark place as oils can go rancid quickly.

Hemp and Flax seed oils are highly nutritious, high in EFA's, are great in salads and recipes but they are more expensive and used more as supplements. Both of these oils should be stored in the fridge.

Sesame oil – The most common type is toasted sesame oil which is used in a lot of Asian cuisine. It has a very rich distinctive flavor which is hard to translate using raw ingredients. This can be found in most supermarkets. There is raw sesame oil, which is much lighter in color and flavor and very hard to find. It is sometimes used in East Indian cuisine and can be found mostly in Indian shops.

Olives – are highly nutritious, but cannot be eaten straight from trees. They all need to be cured first in a brine solution for several days and then they are packed in a way to retain (or add to) their flavor. Olives are then generally either marinated in oil, canned or pickled in vinegar or sun-dried. Bottled and canned olives are processed and cooked. The difference between the green ones and black ones is that the black are riper. Green olives are picked while young and unripe and are therefore generally more bitter and dense.

 – is the husks of psyllium seeds which are ground into a powder. The husk is a mucilage - a clear colorless gelling agent, and it is hydrophilic, meaning it attracts and binds to water. It is tasteless and is used as a thickener in many raw recipes.

Salt - Recipes asking for Salt are always referring to a high quality natural salt, such as **Himalayan salt** or **Celtic sea salt**, which is hand harvested and sun dried. Freshly ground Celtic salt is my preference; it is mineral rich, containing over 80 minerals, including calcium. These salts not only taste amazing, they usually contain a much lower level of sodium. Bleached white table salt is harmful to us but pure, natural salt can be good for you, balancing our systems, homeostasis, when used in moderation. Salt is beneficial in gourmet recipes also as it brings the flavor out in food.

Sea Vegetables – are extremely mineral rich and nutrient dense and are effective in the diet in small amounts. Ideally they should be consumed in small doses but regularly in meals. Many sea vegetables are roasted; look specifically for ones that are dried.

These are some of the more popular types:

Arame and **Hijiki** – are both small black seaweed strands which are sold dried and reconstituted by soaking in water. They have a very mild taste and are nutritionally dense.

Dulse – Many people eat dulse, as it is sold in its dried form, as a salty snack. Dulse powder and flakes are often used as a condiment and sprinkled on salads and other dishes.

Irish moss – Has almost no flavor and is used for its gelatinous quality as a thickening agent in recipes, mainly desserts. It is its carrageenan which is often used in many vegetarian soy-based products.

Kelp powder or **flakes** – dried and shredded or powdered.

Kelp noodles – Clear, long spaghetti shaped noodles made of kelp with very little taste. They are available from the Sea Tangle kelp noodle company.

Kombu - is similar to, in appearance, taste and nutritionally, but not as popular as, wakame. It is often used in soups and stocks. It contains glutamic acid, a natural flavor enhancer, which encouraged researchers to develop a synthetic form - monosodium glutamate (MSG).

Nori –This is what is used in most sushi. Nori grows like a sea lettuce but we usually find it pressed into sheets. The roasted dark green sheets are commonly found in most supermarkets but the dried black nori can be harder to find. Goldmine makes high-quality dried nori sheets (see Resources).

Wakame – is a dark green sea vegetable used mainly in soups and salads. It is commonly found in miso soup. This highly nutritious fern-like sea vegetable grows on the ocean floor. It contains alginic acid which is said to bond with heavy metals and remove them from the body. It is sold dried and must be soaked before using.

Spices – As opposed to herbs which are the flavorful green leaves of plants, spices, usually used in dried form, come from the roots, seeds, fruit and bark of a plant, which is often tropical. Buy quality organic spices. While ordinary non-organic spices bought from the grocery store may be used it is good to be aware that they may contain sugar and artificial sweeteners and colors, MSG, preservatives, corn starch, potato flour, citric acid or other ingredients. They also have a higher chance of being old or rancid. Like herbs, they are often sprayed and irradiated after with harmful chemicals and gasses. Some crops are sprayed more than others, such as peppers. Always buy organic cayenne when possible! My favorite spices are cardamom, chili, cinnamon, cumin, curry, and cayenne.

Spice Blends can be handy to have premade. If you really want to have a culinary experience you can experiment with creating your own blends. Many typical and traditional blends can vary greatly according to region and personal preference.

These are some popular and commonly used spice blends
Cajun and **Creole** – Chili powder, Paprika, Onion powder, Basil, Oregano, Coriander, Thyme, Cumin, Black pepper and Cayenne pepper
Chinese 5 Spice – Cinnamon, Cloves, Fennel, Anise and Szechwan peppercorns
Curry – Coriander, Cumin, Turmeric and Fenugreek
Garam Masala – Cloves, Cardamom, Cinnamon, Nutmeg and Black Pepper (which should only be added to the mixture if used immediately). Other spices sometimes added include: Fennel, Cumin, Mustard seed, Turmeric, dried Ginger, dried Garlic, Bay leaves, dried Red Chillies, and Star Anise.
Greek - Oregano, Garlic, Onion, Parsley, Cinnamon, and Nutmeg
Italian – Oregano, Rosemary, Basil, Marjoram, Thyme and Sage.
Mexican – Chili powder, Cumin, Onion powder, Oregano, dried Garlic
Stuffing Mix – Sage, Thyme, Onion powder, Black pepper, Paprika

Tahini – is the ground paste of sesame seeds, which is highly nutritious, rich in minerals and vitamins, including the B vitamins, and a natural protein source. It can be eaten as a spread, as is, or mixed with other ingredients to make delicious dips, spreads, snacks and is used in many other recipes. It can be blended with water to make sesame milk. Tahini is a traditional food used in various cultures around the world for thousands of years. Make sure when buying it that it is organic and raw.

Tamarind - is a brown plump legume, with as brown brittle skin which looks like large snap beans. You can tell they are mature the skin shatters by squeezing with your fingers. Inside is a honey-colored, gummy mass inside with several very hard seeds the size of baby lima beans. Tamarind can be a lot of work to use but it has a delicious and unique flavor which makes it totally worth it. Tamarind can be bought in most Asian grocery stores or markets. It is usually found in a 7 oz - 1"x 2 ½ "x 3" block. To use make into a paste by placing the block in a dish of water, enough to cover and let soak for a while, at least half an hour. Then when it is soft, I mash it up using a fork or my fingers (it gets quite messy) until it gets pasty and the seeds are loosened. Then press this paste through a small metal strainer, stirring and pressing against the inside with a spoon. Now you have a tamarind paste.

Umeboshi Plums – are an ancient medicinal food which is very alkalizing. These plums are known for treating nausea and they are known to stimulate the digestive system and promote the elimination of toxins. Japanese plums are green and turn red by being pickled with red shiso leaves. Umeboshi plum paste is versatile and easy to use, but you can also often find the plums, bottles in a brine solution, and umeboshi vinegar at most health food stores. Buy a quality brand paste which is pureed, some non-raw concentrates are made by boiling down the plums.

Vanilla – Beans can be expensive and harder to find but are worth it for the flavor. They are the healthiest and the best raw choice. The more popular, cheaper and easier alternative is vanilla extract in which the flavor is extracted from the bean and bottled. As it is so much more common I used extract measurements in recipes. To use the bean (1" = 1 t) often the bean is cut open and the tiny seeds inside are scraped out to use. These seeds contain the most and best flavor but the pod can also be ground and used.

Vinegar - Apple cider vinegar is the only raw vinegar. When buying, look for one with the mother culture in it. Balsamic vinegar is made from grapes and aged. It has a distinctive flavor but is not raw and is quite acidic. All vinegars contain acetic acid which is toxic; for health reasons, use any vinegar in moderation. Apple cider and umeboshi plum vinegars have the lowest acid levels.

9 INDEX

D

F

G

H

ABOUT THE AUTHOR

Robin Gregory has been creating delicious raw food recipes and working as a consultant in the raw and living foods field for over seven years. She has developed recipes, products and designed menu plans for several raw restaurants and has been actively involved in the center of the raw community. Robin now works freelance as a restaurant start-up consultant and with individuals in various health related areas, from nutrition to cleanses to alternative health counselling and fitness.

Join Robin on her website, Robins Key www.robinskey.com, to see new recipes as they are developed and created. These ultra-healthy recipes are regularly posted, along with all of her favorite strategies to achieve a strong, fit body and optimal health. Robins Key is filled with delicious recipes, creative workouts and inspiration to motivate you to be the best *you* possible!

5414678R00086

Made in the USA
San Bernardino, CA
05 November 2013